Sophie Murphy Does Not Exist

T. Blanchard

CHICKEN SCRATCH BOOKS

WWW.CHICKENSCRATCHBOOKS.COM

Chicken Scratch Books
PO Box 104
Wisdom, MT 59761

www.chickenscratchbooks.com

Publisher's Note: This is a work of fiction. Names, characters, places, and incidents are a product of the author's imagination. Locales and public names are sometimes used for atmospheric purposes. Any resemblance to actual people, living or dead, or to businesses, companies, events, institutions, or locales is completely coincidental.

Ordering Information: Special discounts are available on quantity purchases by corporations, associations, and others. For details, contact the publisher at the address above.

First Chicken Scratch Books Printing, 2021

ISBN 978-1-953743-02-2 (paperback)
ISBN 978-1-953743-03-9 (ebook)

Printed in the United States of America

For Mr. McGregor,

my sixth grade teacher at Thatcher Elementary,

who planted the writing seed.

And for Troy,

who nourished it.

Contents

CHAPTER 1

Lemons

My dad promised that it didn't hurt to die but I'm pretty sure he was lying. I may find out for myself today because my head really aches. I drag myself from my bedroom to the kitchen where I almost crash into Grandma Charlotte. I call her GC whenever my dad isn't around to protest that it's disrespectful. I guess I can call her GC all the time now, but it's sort of lost its zing for me. It's hard to break old habits though.

It's only eight in the morning, but Grandma's lips are already outlined with pink peony lipstick and her nose is powdered. She's putting blueberry muffins in the oven. I wait for the door to clang shut and then I give GC a quick hug. I include a groan, not that it's necessary, but it gets her attention.

GC stops humming. "What's the matter, sweet pea? Come here and let me have a look?" She tosses flowered oven mitts onto the counter and cups my face in her warm hands. I close my eyes and inhale lemons and blueberry muffins. The cheerful smell of my Grandma floats through the house when she visits. After she leaves, it will linger in the spare bedroom and I will go there to breathe her again.

"I am relatively sure that I have meningitis," I say. "And you know meningitis in teenagers is deadly."

GC crinkles her forehead. "Good thing you're not a teenager until March." She sticks her head into the hallway. "Alex! Your daughter isn't feeling well!"

The muffins are cooling on the counter when my mother finally pads into the kitchen. She does not smell like lemons. Her brown hair, which is usually smooth, pokes in every direction. She probably went to bed with her hair wet. Mom's been taking long showers at night. Maybe she thinks we can't hear her crying in there.

"What illness do you have now, Sophie?"

"Meningitis. The deadly kind."

She puts her hand on my forehead and I will myself to have a fever. "No fever. I think you'll live."

As usual, my body has failed me.

"Don't you think it's time to go back to school? You are falling behind."

I don't answer, because I know GC will rush to my aid.

She doesn't fail me. "Alexandra. It's only been two weeks. Sophie needs more time." GC eyes Mom's hair and stained paisley bathrobe. "Look at you. You're not exactly ready to face the world either."

Mom starts to protest but GC shoots her down. "And no one expects you to. But you can't expect Sophie to adjust more easily than you have."

I love Grandma Charlotte. I hope she never goes home to Minnesota. Her stay has been the only good thing that's happened in the last few weeks.

Mom sighs heavily, her morning breath as stinky and hot as the exhaust from my school bus. "All right. I don't have the energy to fight both of you." She flops back to her bedroom, where I expect she will stay for the next eight hours.

I grab a blueberry muffin and the newspaper from the counter and try not to gloat at my victory. It's hard though because victories are rare when Mom is in the mix.

"Where are the obituaries?" I ask GC.

She freezes, which is a sign because GC moves constantly. If she stops moving, I know she's either asleep or guilty. "I threw that section away."

"But GC, I've read the obituaries every morning since Dad got sick."

GC shoves a bowl in the dishwasher. "It's time to stop reading those, Sophie. It's not healthy."

I open the trash can and carefully shake eggshells from Section E. "I'm all right. And didn't Dr. Williams say we should keep things consistent?"

Dr. Williams is my therapist. I'm not happy about being forced to "visit" with him every week, but mom said it was important to talk to someone about my *feelings*. "I'll just talk to you and GC," I'd said, but she insisted that it had to be a professional.

GC gives up. She and I both know that she can't fight Dr. Williams. She snaps open a can of Dr. Pepper, grabs a muffin and Section A, and settles into a chair at the kitchen table. She's a headline type: glances at the lead stories, too busy to bother with the guts of the paper.

I sit two chairs away, leaving enough space to spread out the newspaper. I read the first name on the page. Warren Butterfield. Died at age 83. Leaves behind 3 children, 8 grandchildren, and 2 great-grandchildren.

The obituaries are listed alphabetically in the *Gilbert Times*. I suppose they couldn't list them any other way, like age at death or order of importance. I imagine families lining up outside the newspaper office, waving signs and chanting. "Obits are worst. Grandpa Warren should be first."

I scan through the listings, turn the page and stop. National Obituaries. Why haven't I noticed these before? Have I always stopped after the locals? Has my world been that small?

Nina Ivanov, ballet dancer at the National Ballet Company, says page 8. *Theodore Young, composer.*

They actually *do* segregate the important people from the common ones. Just like they did on the Titanic. First-class important people get the upper decks and the National page. Second class regular people go down with the ship.

"What is the difference between the national obituaries and the local?" I ask GC.

"Hmmm?" She looks up.

I repeat my question.

She has obviously not thought of it before. "I guess national obituaries are published...well, nationally, for people who have accomplished something on a national level."

I think of my dad's obituary. Not surprisingly I have it memorized, and I can review the key points quickly. Michael Murphy, age 41. Lost his valiant fight with cancer on September 25. Beloved husband, father, son.

He was listed only in the local obituaries because he did not do anything really important. He was a dentist. Because he lived, people had better teeth. He made a difference to Mrs. Foster's molars.

And to me.

CHAPTER 2

Baby Shampoo

"Do we have to watch this every morning?" I yell to Grandma Charlotte when the TV interrupts my research.

"A good day always begins with *The Price is Right*."

I figure I owe her one. She lets me read obituaries, I let her watch Drew Carey give away cars.

"$24.99!" GC shouts at the screen. "Everyone knows the retail price of a Hamilton Beach coffee maker is $24.99."

"Thirty-two dollars," guesses the contestant.

GC sighs and drops to the sofa. "Where do they find these people?"

The Price is Right may not be educational, but it is a good alarm clock. My four-year-old brother Oliver wanders into the living room rubbing his eyes. He avoids Grandma's price drama and comes to my couch. I hold out my arms and pull him onto my lap. He is still sleepy, so he accepts the cuddle. I bury my nose in his hair and breathe in the sweet smell of baby shampoo. The world would be a much better place if it just smelled like GC and Ollie.

"Mom?" he asks.

"Bed." I reach out to smooth his soft hair before he can push my hand away.

He doesn't even ask for Dad, who is usually at work by the time Ollie wakes up. I'm not sure Ollie realizes that Dad is permanently gone.

When both contestants overbid their showcases, GC sighs. "I am finished with this show."

I know better. She's only finished until it comes on again tomorrow morning. If she gave up on it completely, she'd miss a contestant bidding the exact price of a showcase. She can't give it up cold turkey any easier than I could give up on the obituaries.

Ollie and I settle in to watch the next show: *The Young and the Old*, or something like that. We'd both rather watch something else, but I don't see the remote and I'm too lazy to pull the cushions off the couch to look for it.

"I enjoy life because I take Catadyle for my high blood pressure," says a grey-haired man in the next commercial. *Whatever*, I silently tell him. *Your happiness is temporary. You may not die from high blood pressure, but you'll die from Mad Cow Disease or Fish Odor Syndrome.*

Undeterred by my mental warnings, a smiley lady shaving her legs pops onto the screen. I remember her. She's Callie Owen, a gold medalist at the Olympics last summer. She'd be on the National page if she died. The story would be all over the news, with somber-faced reporters talking about how much she meant to so many and what a tragedy her death was. People would probably build make-shift shrines. They'd pile teddy bears and daisies on the sidewalk in front of her house and leave with tears running down their cheeks.

I scoot Ollie off my lap, dig out the remote and find a cartoon train show. Ollie doesn't notice when I leave the room.

Dad's den sits dark and empty. Like me, it's waiting for him to walk through the door whistling a Tim McGraw song. I pull open the blinds and try to whistle, but the air refuses to move. I wonder if the air inside a coffin is this still.

I hear another commercial blaring from the family room and remember why I wandered into his den. I turn on the computer and type Callie Owen in the search bar. A Netopedia listing pops up first. I'm not surprised, because Netopedia knows everything about everyone important. It says Callie is nineteen years old and lives with her parents and sister in Columbus, Ohio.

I think about her as I stare out the front window.

GC must have remembered that today is garbage day because two gray bins sit in front of our house. The street is quiet and, except for the bins, empty. I don't see even one teddy bear.

People remembered garbage day, but not my dad.

I run to the kitchen, grab Section E, and scurry back to Dad's den. Nina Ivanov the ballerina. She has a page. Theodore Young the composer. He's there too.

I type in my dad's name and count forty-nine Michael Murphys. They are singers, hockey players, politicians. But no dentists.

Even if he was only a dad and a dentist, the world is worse without him. If he's not important enough to be listed in the National obituaries, at least he could have a Netopedia page.

I read the instructions and email Netopedia a paragraph about my dad.

Dear Netopedia:

I noticed that you're missing a listing of one of the most important people in the world. Except he's not in the world anymore. He was born in Flagstaff, Arizona, and went to dental school in Kansas. He had three brothers and three kids. But that's not what makes him important. The most important things are that he practiced whistling a lot. He remembered people. Not just their teeth, but their names and their favorite movies. He made my mom smile when no one else could, and he told really dumb jokes. He coached his son's baseball team and his daughter's soccer team, and not because he knew anything about baseball or soccer. His name is Michael Murphy. You should include him in your listings. Preferably first.

Thanks for your attention to this matter,

Sophie Murphy

I press send and listen to the swoosh sound as it flies through space.

And then I type my name. I already know what the result will be but I can't resist.

"Sophie Murphy does not exist," says Netopedia.

I don't even bother to email Netopedia to tell them they're wrong.

When I die (which may be soon, given my headache), my obituary will be on the local page. I think of what it will say.

Sophie Hannah Murphy, age 12. Daughter of Alexandra and Michael, sister to Oliver and Trevor, granddaughter of Charlotte. Friend of Mia, Jessie, and Ashley. Girlfriend of no one ever. Average student. Average soccer player. Made decent macaroni and cheese from a box. Teddy bears and other small tokens may be left at 2232 Mesa Verde Drive in Gilbert, Arizona.

Who am I kidding? There wouldn't be any teddy bears. I am even more ordinary than my dad. He was on the local page. I wouldn't even be a blurb. Neither of us is Netopedia worthy.

If I am ever going to exist, at least where it really matters, I've got to do something really important. Something that makes my mark.

Something that means something to someone.

CHAPTER 3

Day 1 Of A New Normal

Mom flips on my light at 6:00 a.m., which is basically the middle of the night, as far as I'm concerned. "Time for school!" she announces, too bright, too early. She leans to brush the hair from my face and I smell toothpaste. I sit up in bed and stare at her. *I smell toothpaste.* I thought she stopped brushing her teeth a week ago.

"I can't go to school. I'm highly contagious," I tell her. "I have dengue fever."

Mom raises her eyebrows. "Dengue fever?"

I nod. I read about it last night and I have all the symptoms.

"You think you have dengue fever, transmitted by mosquitoes, usually found in tropical climates?"

I sigh, defeated. I thought I picked a disease she wouldn't know anything about. "Or something like dengue. Some horrible, contagious disease that is *not* transmitted by mosquitoes."

I grab at the comforter, but she pulls it away. "Come on, Sophie. Get in the shower."

As the water beats down on my skin, I think my life would be much easier if my mom were not a nurse. Why could I not have been born to an accountant or a garbage collector? Or maybe a guitar teacher, who makes flower wreaths for my hair and plays love songs.

At least I am the granddaughter of a cook. GC has made celebratory (or maybe they are condolence) waffles for breakfast. I grab the can of whip cream and bury my waffle under beautiful sticky foam.

"Where's Trevor?" I ask GC. Trevor is my sixteen-year-old brother. He hasn't been home since he was twelve. That's an exaggeration, but only a little one. I think he still sleeps here but the last time I saw him was at Dad's funeral. Basically, Dad got sick and Trevor moved out.

GC shakes her head. "Trevor's gone."

It doesn't matter anyway because Trevor would never be seen riding to school with me and GC. It would decrease his cool factor by at least eighty degrees.

GC drives me. I could catch the bus, but riding the bus and sitting through Math seems like way too much activity for a girl who may have a disease that resembles dengue.

"Thanks, GC." I lean over to squeeze her before I jump out of the car.

GC rolls down the window. "Go get 'em kiddo," she calls. I give her thumbs up and walk through the front door where Carter Griffin is standing. I look away before he spots me staring at him. It's hard to watch him covertly without tripping.

Carter Griffin may be the only good thing about middle school. He's the most beautiful boy I've ever seen. I gazed at the freckles dotting his nose during the first five weeks of sixth grade. He hasn't talked to me yet, but I have high hopes.

"And Sophie Murphy is here," a booming voice calls like it's narrating a movie.

"Hello, Mr. Gomez." I almost forgot about the assistant principal. The man must lie in bed at night and study the yearbook because he knows the name of every student at Treasure Valley Middle School. He demonstrates his knowledge from the same spot every morning. The poor man needs another hobby.

"How are you?"

"I'm fine, Mr. Gomez."

"You sure?" He studies my face, concern in his eyes, and I just want to run away. *This* is the reason I've been avoiding school. I can't take the sympathy.

"You're back!" Jessie interrupts Mr. Gomez. She grabs my arm and pulls me toward Mia. "Look, Sophie's back!"

Mia pulls a binder from her locker. "Hey, Sophie. We've missed you at lunch." It's a sweet thing to say, but I suspect she missed me because I give her half of my desserts. She misses my brownies. Me, not so much.

I'm not sure what I expected, but apparently, life really does go on at Treasure Valley Middle. Other than my friends and Mr. Gomez, no one even acknowledges that I was gone for three weeks, or cares about why. I trudge through six classes and collect all of my accumulated homework.

When I get home, I notice that even our house has moved on. A vase of cheerful daisies sits on the kitchen table and sunshine streams in the windows. Stupid sunshine. It's always around, even when you don't want it. I march through the house and close every curtain and blind until the rooms feel dark and gloomy, the way they should.

I sit on my bed and hum *Live Like You Were Dying*. It was Dad's favorite Tim McGraw song, and he sang it up until he actually was.

Dying I mean.

CHAPTER 4

Day 2. Fruits

On Day 2 of "normal," I wake up without an appetite. I inform Mom and GC that I have symptoms of Beaver Fever, but my mother ignores all the signs and forces me to school anyway. Jessie isn't in Language Arts, and I don't see any of my other friends at lunchtime. There is nothing worse than standing in the middle of the cafeteria by yourself, looking for a place to sit, so I plop into the nearest empty seat. It happens to be at the popular girls' table.

Emily Partridge sits at the center, holding court. I know Emily. She was in my third and fourth-grade classes at Sand Point Elementary. She was beautiful then too, but less so. Now her streaked blond hair falls in waves down her back and she's dressed like an Abercrombie & Fitch model. I doubt she's ever felt awkward; I know she's never looked it. Even with braces, when every other teenager looks ridiculous, she's still beautiful.

"We have to decide on our costumes for Halloween," Emily tells the five girls who sit on either side and across from her.

I sit at the end of their table, leaving a little space between us. They don't acknowledge that I am there, but at least they don't tell me to get lost.

"I think we should all be different colors," says Zoe. "Like crayons."

"No." Emily rejects the idea outright, and Zoe looks crushed. "That is really juvenile."

"How about Star Wars costumes? You could be Princess Leia and we could be...the other guys," offers another girl I don't know.

"If you want to match the nerds," says Zoe. She looks at me, and then to Emily for confirmation.

"How about fruits?" says Lauren. She points. "You could be an apple, you a banana, you a grape..."

"Sure," says Emily. "If you want to be ugly and fat for the day." She spots me. I'm biting a carrot stick when I feel her eyes on me. The table is quiet.

"Hi ahh... What's your name again?"

I look up to see them all staring at me. "Sophie. Sophie Murphy." I stammer.

"Oh, yeah, I know you," she says and I relax a little. Of course she knows me. We've been in the same schools since kindergarten.

"Yeah, my homeroom teacher told us to be *kind* to you." She turns to Zoe, who's sitting next to her. "Don't you think it's lame when teachers try to tell us who to be friends with? Like we can't choose on our own? And we have to be nice to *someone* just because her dad died? Like, big deal. People die all the time. My grandma died two years ago."

I stare at the lunch table, willing myself to shrink down into one of the molecules in the wood grain. I don't. And I'm stuck in this seat because I'm afraid if I make a move I'll open a flood of tears that are temporarily dammed. Dammed tears.

"I think we should be tourists." She's moved on, thank goodness.

It's pretty obvious, to me at least, that she wants to dress as a tourist so that she can wear shorts. I'm sure her legs are golden tan and worthy of showing off. I suddenly hope it's freezing on Halloween. I hope it's freezing and Emily's mom forces her to wear long sweat pants and a jacket. Or better yet, a snowsuit. I imagine the thought of Emily and her friends waddling down the street in snowsuits. The thought distracts me momentarily, and I smile.

Emily eyes me again. "Sophie, right? What are you going to be for Halloween?"

I feel the heat of twelve eyes. They're looking at me again. Can they just stop looking at me?

"I...ummm... I forgot about Halloween. I was Joan of Arc last year. This year I'll probably just stay home and hand out candy."

"Oh," Emily blinks. "You were Joe from where? Is that from a movie?"

"It doesn't really matter," says Zoe, touching Emily's arm as if she's trying to call Emily's attention back to her. "What about your party? Is Matt coming with his friends?"

A gagging hiccup sound from the left corner of the lunchroom interrupts them. I turn in time to see Paul Weir sprint to the garbage can with his hand over his mouth. He doesn't make it before he spews his lunch. The stench of vomit fills the air.

I instruct my stomach to stay calm, but my stomach is a long way from my head and the instructions take too long to get there. I jump up, grab my lunch tray, and head for the door, gagging as I go.

I knew I was getting sick. I could feel it coming on. I'm so sick I can't even hang around for my social studies test. I walk to the nurse's office, where I see Paul sitting on a chair, his head stuck in a trash bin between his knees.

"I'll just wait in the hall," I tell the nurse. "It looks like you have some germs in here." Paul lifts his head and I grimace sympathetically. I understand his pain. He groans and puts his head back in the trash bin. His skin is the strange color of pea soup.

CHAPTER 5

Day 2 (continued).
Fish Sticks + Vomit

GC arrives at the nurse's office to rescue me. "Oh Sophie, you look like death warmed over," she says as she pats my arm.

She freezes. "Oh darlin, that was insensitive. I shouldn't have mentioned death. It fell outta my mouth before my brain could catch it."

I climb into the van. "It's ok GC. We can't all be blessed with social grace."

When she pulls into the garage, I slide open the minivan door, run into the house and head straight for the bathroom. I gaze in the mirror to see if I look as green as Paul. My face looks pink, as usual, but when I open my mouth to check out my tonsils I see a tinge of green. I knew it.

"Are you hungry?" GC calls.

"Not right now," I answer, remembering the smell of fish sticks mixed with vomit. "Maybe later."

I shuffle to my bedroom, flop on my bed, and stare at the ceiling.

"Sophie! Dinner!" GC calls after a while. My stomach growls, so I haul myself to the kitchen. "What's for dinner?"

GC smiles wickedly. "Tater tot casserole."

"GC! You made *that* for an invalid? On the same day I smelled vomit?" It's an insult. It's almost like she doesn't believe that I am deathly ill.

"It's *comfort food,* Sophie. Try it." She hands me a plate with two scoops of tater tot casserole.

"This is not your best work," I tell GC when I'm on my third helping. "I'm just eating it to keep my strength up."

GC snorts.

I fill the dishwasher, and, my strength restored, I head to Dad's den and click the computer to life. *New message from Netopedia,* my email says. I click it.

Dear Submitter,
Netopedia is the top source of reliable information on the internet. We receive thousands of submissions each week, and we are

therefore limited in the listings we choose to publish.

We must reject your submission. We cannot publish the biographies of persons who are not notable or in whom the public has no interest. As a rule, if no general publication newspaper or magazine has published an article about the person which can be referenced, the person is not suitable Netopedia material.

Thank you for your interest in our site.

Sincerely,

The Netopedia Staff

I read it again, and even a third time to make sure. He's not suitable Netopedia material? If he was a singer, hockey player, or politician, he'd be notable. But "the public" has no interest in the Michael Murphy who was only a dad and dentist.

How do you *Live Like You Were Dying?* How do you become interesting and important enough to exist at Treasure Valley Middle and in Netopedia-land?

SOPHIE MURPHY DOES NOT EXIST.

Netopedia is right. Even people I've gone to school with for the last seven years don't remember my name. I've got to do something so they *want* to know me. I've got to do something so all of these people *beg* to hang out with me. I've got to do something *notable*.

Because here's the thing: my Dad's dead. His chance is gone, he can't change anything about his life now. But I can. I'm still alive, at least for now. I've got to make my mark. The problem is... on what?

CHAPTER 6

Day 2 (continued again). Possibilities

I take a deep breath. When I feel overwhelmed by something, I make a list. I figured that out on my own a few weeks ago without any help, even from Dr. Williams-the-therapist. He's not great at giving practical suggestions.

I figured out that sometimes you have to take things day by day. You have to take a thing that seems huge and break it into small parts. *If you want to eat an elephant, you take small bites*, as GC says. Although I don't know why anyone would want to eat an elephant, ever. That sounds horribly disgusting. And sad.

I rummage through my desk drawer, pull out my LISTS notebook, and turn to the first page, where I've already written three rules.

Practical Rules for Life

1. *When you feel overwhelmed by a huge thing, break it into baby things.*
2. *Be prepared. Surprises usually don't turn out well.*
3. *Do not eat 5 corndogs and then go to bed.*

I add some things that suddenly seem terribly important.

4. *Do not, under any circumstance, ever eat an elephant. Even if you're on an African safari and the only dinner choices are hedgehogs or elephants.*
5. *If you want to be remembered after you die, you have to do something important while you're alive.*

I stare at Rule Five for a minute, and then I turn to an empty page and write.

Becoming Netopedia Notable.

I look at the long list of Michael Murphys who <u>are</u> notable enough to be listed and start with the things they did.

1. Politician

I strike that pretty fast. First, I've never even considered running for student council. Mario Sanchez is the seventh-grade class president. He's friendly and smiley and I don't think I have that in me. Second, I am too young to run for something important, like the Mayor of Gilbert or Senator of Arizona. Those people are *old*. Third, it sounds pretty boring. What does a politician even do besides waving at parades from the back of a convertible? Fourth: I don't even remember the name of the Vice-President of the United States. He's pretty high up there and not even famous.

2. Hockey player

The likelihood of me achieving fame in the hockey rink is zero. The last time I went to the ice-skating rink, I used a skating walker doohickey the entire time. And I live in Arizona. Enough said about that. Moving on.

3. Singer

That is a possibility. I have a pretty good voice, at least when I sing in the shower. I may be a little afraid of singing by myself on stage, but I've been to a few concerts and seen some videos and people singing on TV. They all had dancers and backup singers, so I won't even be singing alone.

Dad taught me to play the G and D chords on the guitar, and I can always carry it to show I'm a serious musician. Besides, lots of teenagers were discovered from YouTube videos. How hard could it be?

But I'm scared. I've never sung on my own before, and the thought of singing on stage (even with the backup singers and dancers) freaks me out a little.

I need to think about this. The odds of success of all three of these seem pretty low.

CHAPTER 7

Day 3. Candyblox

It usually takes 11 minutes to drive to Treasure Valley Middle. If GC is driving, it takes approximately 7.5. Today, half of the lanes are blocked by orange barrels, so the lines are long and slow.

"Grams, can I play Candyblox on your phone?" Ollie calls from the back seat. GC fishes in her sparkly purple purse and passes it back to him. He's content until the phone buzzes.

"I got it," he calls.

"You're four," she mutters. "How can you work my phone better than I can?"

"Hello," Ollie says into the phone.

"Mrs. Taylor?" Ollie has answered on speaker.

"Yes?" GC yells from the front seat while trying to maneuver around a Chevrolet turning left.

"This is Mike Brown from KTVU News in Minneapolis. You're a hard lady to track down.

We're doing a feature story, called 'Where are they now?' that I'd like you to be part of. We'd like to bring a camera crew..."

GC yanks the steering wheel to the right and pulls between construction cones. She takes the phone from Ollie, punches the speaker off, and puts the phone to her ear.

"Mister... what did you say your name is? Mr. Brown. I appreciate you thinkin' of me..."

She listens. "It's been a long time since I even thought about that....No, can't say that I have."

A construction worker approaches the van. GC waves him off. "No, I don't think so. Bye now."

I wait until we've pulled out of the construction zone. "GC? Who was that?"

"No one of consequence." She stares at the road, a million miles away.

She's hiding something.

But why?

"GC," I try again. "Why is a news guy calling you? Are you famous?"

The van screeches to a stop in front of the school. "Nope. Have a great day, Sweet Pea."

I grab my backpack. "You have no idea?"

"Scoot along, darlin. I've got cars waiting behind me."

She hardly even waits for me to shut the door behind me, and she's gone.

I don't have to be a genius to deduce that something is going on. I trudge impatiently through my classes and resist the temptation to visit the school nurse to tell her about the bump on the knuckle of my left hand. As soon as the last bell rings, I race outside to meet GC.

"GC, we need to talk," I say as I slam the van door closed.

She rolls her eyes, which I ignore. Sometimes GC has a bad attitude.

"What's going on? Why did that guy call you this morning?"

"How was your day?"

"GC. Don't avoid the question. Answer me." I sound a little like my mother, which is a horrifying thought.

"Sophie. Don't you worry your little head about it. Mind your own biscuits and life will be gravy."

As soon as we get home, I rush to the computer and type Charlotte Taylor into the search bar. There are approximately ten pages of Charlotte Taylors. I find the Charlotte Taylor who belongs to me on a page describing her term as the Blooming Violets Gardening Club President. I briefly wonder if that's her secret past, but I'm pretty sure KTVU

News would not do a story to update us on the past presidents of a gardening club.

There has to be something else. I type her maiden name. Charlotte Morgan. Three listings, but nothing that might match my Charlotte Morgan Taylor.

GC must have done something to make her famous. Something she refuses to talk about. I decide to leave her secret buried for now. But patience is not one of my strengths and I'm not sure how long I can wait for answers.

CHAPTER 8

Day 5. Lasagna

"How was your day?" GC asks when she picks me up after school on Friday.

"The same. Unremarkable. Boring." I notice that we are not driving in the direction of my house. "Where are we going?"

"Mighty Mart." Grandma guns the minivan through a yellow light. "I need mozzarella cheese to make lasagna for dinner."

I have no objection to that. I'm willing to do anything for lasagna, even drive to the grocery store after school. We pass Dad's dental office on Riverside Drive, but something about it looks very odd.

"Who is Dr. Dolittle and why is his sign up at Dad's office?"

"He must be the dentist who bought your Dad's practice," answers Grandma.

"What?" It comes out louder than I expected.

"When your Dad got sick, they started looking for someone who could take over his office," GC says calmly. "Looks like they found someone."

My Dad's office has been in the same strip mall, with the same receptionist and the same sign since I was seven years old. And two weeks after he dies, Dr. Doolittle just walks in and takes over where my dad left off? There is no downtime, no missing him. Dad disappears and a replacement pops up. Mrs. Foster's molars won't even realize that a different dentist is in charge.

If I died, nothing in the world would change. No molars would rot, no office signs would change. I sink down in my seat and consider Netopedia. If everyone who is anyone is listed, then I have to figure out a way to get on there. Someone has to realize when I'm gone.

I prop my leg on the dashboard and stare at the stub.

Stub. Razors. Callie Owen's face on the commercial pops into my head.

"Callie Owen!" I shout as the answer comes to me.

"What?"

"Do you know who that is?" It's a test.

"The Olympic gymnast?" Even GC, who watches nothing on TV except *The Price is Right* and reads only the headlines on the front page knows Callie Owen. Everyone knows Callie Owen. *I am going to be* Callie Owen.

Now it seems so obvious.

"I need to sign up for gymnastics," I say. "Right now, there's not a minute to spare."

"It can't wait for lasagna?"

"Lasagna is pretty much the highlight of my life," I admit. "All right. Mighty Mart first, then gymnastics."

We find a gym a few blocks from the grocery store. GC talks to the coach and I watch the gymnasts. As I watch, my confidence drips like a popsicle at noon. I dreamed about being a gymnast in second grade when I was the best cartwheeler at Sand Point Elementary. But forget cartwheels, these little pipsqueaks can flip and spin and turn like nobody's business. GC pulls me out the door before I even start considering possible injuries.

"I told the coach you are new to gymnastics," GC says to me as we walk to the car. "She said you could try a class next Tuesday with some other beginners."

I won't be a beginner for long, I assure myself, trying to maintain confidence. I refuse to admit, even to myself, that I am a little nervous about wiping out.

Still, while GC's lasagna bakes in the oven that night, I open my LISTS notebook and fill in possibility number *4: Gymnastics*.

It seems so much easier than the other three.

CHAPTER 9

Day 8. Leotards

The weekend passes quickly and it's Monday again before I remember I'm a soon-to-be gymnastics prodigy. "What do gymnasts wear to class?" I ask Jessie at lunch. She takes tap lessons so she should know these things.

"Leotards, of course." She talks with her mouth open and I can see chicken taco all mushed up inside. "Why?"

"I'm going to try a class tomorrow."

"Oh. Do you want to borrow a leotard?"

"No thanks. I'll just wear a t-shirt and soccer shorts," I tell her.

Jessie wrinkles her nose. "You can't move in those. The shirt will fly up as soon as you go upside down."

I hadn't planned to turn upside down. Especially my first day. "I'll wear a swimsuit. It's pretty much the same thing, right?"

"Not at all," says Jessie. "You'll look ridiculous."

I consider that. No sense in looking stupid before I even do a cartwheel.

I beg GC to take me shopping after school. She's much easier to convince than my mom. Mom would have said, "You have to try it before we spend money on the equipment..." but GC doesn't even bat an eyelash when I tell her I need a leotard.

We find lots of dance leotards but only a few for gymnastics. Finally, when I'm about to die of starvation, we find a plain green gymnastics leotard. There are others I like better, like one with blue lightning on it, but I don't want to draw attention to myself yet.

CHAPTER 10

Day 9. Catfish

GC picks me up from school on Tuesday and we head straight to the gym. I change into my leotard in the bathroom, hand my school clothes to GC and stand against the cold cinderblock wall to wait for the class to start. I should have worn my soccer clothes, or at least brought a towel to wrap around myself. I feel naked, standing in what is basically a swimsuit, and I am tired of feeling naked. Stripped of my clothes, stripped of my normal family, stripped of my dignity.

I sniffle a little, but then a lady dressed in a tank and yoga pants yells. "Pop Rocks!"

My stomach flips and I look for the door. I look at Grandma, and she shoos me toward yelling lady. I step onto the floor alone.

"Are you in the Pop Rocks group?" Yelling lady eyes me and folds her arms, which bulge like she's incubating giant ostrich eggs. I take a step back, in case one hatches.

"Um. I guess?" I shrug.

"All right!"

She sounds fake-excited, which makes me suspicious. What are Pop Rocks anyway?

I find out when other girls jump onto the floor, one by one until there are eight of us standing in a line. Eight. One twelve-year-old and seven six-year-olds. I look like a tall weed among multicolored tulips...so much for blending in.

"Class!" Yelling Arm Lady claps her hands, and the class is silent. "This is Sophie. She'll be joining our class."

"You're really tall," one girl says, craning her neck.

"Spread out to stretch." Yelling Arm Lady sinks to the floor, spreads her legs apart, and folds her body in half. Apparently, we are supposed to follow her, because the tulips drop and fold too. I do my best to keep up, but my body doesn't move like that.

"Cartwheels! Line up in three rows." Yelling Arm Lady calls. I take my place at the end of a line at the edge of the bouncy blue floor.

The other pop-rocks spin across the floor and I can hardly tell the difference between their arms and their legs. The tulips are now spindly snowflakes swirling across the ice. I bend to start a cartwheel, but I can't get my legs straight in the air. I do not look like a dancing snowflake. I look like the catfish I caught the last time Dad took me fishing. "I want to keep it," I insisted. It wriggled and gasped on the shore next to me until I couldn't take it anymore and I grabbed it (with my bare hand—uck!) and tossed it back into the water.

Flopping like a catfish was definitely not my plan.

"How long until we do the hard stuff like flips?" I ask Yelling Arm Lady at the end of class. "Like her." I point to a girl on the floor who just backflipped so quickly I couldn't tell how many times she went around.

"She's in level nine," she says. "You're in level... one."

I can accept that I have some room to improve.

"How long will it take to get to Level 9?" I ask. Hopefully, it will be just a few months. The next Olympics is three years away. I've got a little time.

"Girls usually move one level per year, except the higher levels may take longer." She gestures to the flippers. "Those girls practice every day. Twenty-two hours per week."

I almost choke. *"Twenty-two hours a week? For years?"*

I feel my stomach drop. That is a lot of work. Eight years is a long time and a lot of flips. I could be twenty before I got to that level. Twenty is pretty old, and I could die before then.

It'd be an anonymous death.

CHAPTER 11

Day 11. Pop Rocks

I am less than enthusiastic about gymnastics on Thursday.

"Murphys don't quit," GC says when I inform her of my intestinal parasite.

"How do you know? You're not even a Murphy," I point out.

"You've got to give it one more shot."

I bow my head in defeat and shove the ugly green leotard into my backpack.

When Yelling Arm Lady calls for Pop Rocks, I own it. I can be an oversized rock. I can be a boulder. Like Tuesday, we begin with stretching. "It's beam and bars day!" she calls when I am sufficiently stretched out. We head to the beam, which is a narrow piece of wood covered in leather and perched about four feet from the floor. I look at it dubiously, but the little pops jump on it. They take turns walking, holding one leg up, and jumping. I watch them, and every so often I take a step backward toward the exit. Eventually, I might be able to escape unnoticed, although I'm not yet sure how I'll get past GC.

Yelling Arm Lady notices. "Sophie!" she calls. "Your turn!"

"I'm fine here on the floor, thanks. Look, I can do that stuff down here." I start to walk along a white line taped on the floor, but she puts her hands on her hips and glares.

I glance at GC, who brushes her hand at me. I pull myself onto the beam and try slowly walking with my arms stretched out on either side. "Hey," I say, to no one in particular. "This isn't so bad."

"Pull your left leg up behind you and tilt forward," instructs Arms.

I do as she says, my right leg wobbling dangerously.

"Other leg. Good... Both legs on the beam, stand up straight. Now jump into the air and land with both feet on the beam."

Since I was relatively good at balancing on one foot, I try the jump. It does not go as well. I jump into the air. Did I mention that the beam is narrow? I hit it, my legs split apart and I land hard on *that* area between my legs. I collapse forward, stunned and maybe dead, until Yelling Arm Lady uses her bulging arm muscles to lift me to the floor.

I try to stand, but my back stays crooked and my legs stay bowed out. I look like I've been on a three-week horse ride.

The level 9 backflipper walks by and glances at me. "You split the beam. I do that just about every day."

"What?" I sputter. "You go through *this pain* daily?"

"Yep," she laughs, her curly red hair bouncing. I watch as she leaps into the air, grabs a bar, and starts swinging. How is she still moving?

"Pop rocks to the floor!" Yelling Arm Lady gestures to the bouncy floor. The tulips run. I hobble.

"Summersaults!" Luckily I can do those. Well, I can do one or two. Maybe even three or four. After seven, my head is jumbled. I land the eighth on top of a tulip. I unwind in the middle of the turn and my legs slam down on her back.

"Sorry," I call in her direction. I can't see her clearly because the room is spinning.

She giggles. "It's ok, Sophie."

"What's your name?" I ask her.

"I'm Lilly."

"Oh," I say. "Nice to meet you. Sorry about smashing you."

"It's ok," Lilly smiles. "I've got to go. My brother's here."

I watch her step off the bouncy floor and walk to the exit. *Where Carter Griffin is waiting.* He waves cheerfully and I shrink into the floor. My sight is still a little fuzzy, but I'm almost positive he's laughing.

"Maybe gymnastics isn't my sport," I tell GC on the way home.

We stop behind a red convertible at a stoplight. The light changes but the convertible doesn't move. GC honks the horn, waits half a second, then sticks her head out the window.

"Move, you old geezer!" she yells. "I haven't got all day." The horn blares again.

My body is sore, but it moves well enough to get me to the floor of the minivan, where I stay until we pull into the safety of the garage.

CHAPTER 12

Day 12. Silt

"Hey Pop Rock!" calls Carter when I walk into Social Studies. I want to kick him in the shin, but I'd probably get in trouble, and I don't want to give him the satisfaction.

"Today," Mrs. Bowen reminds us, "we're talking about the Nile River and the importance it played to the civilization which became Egypt. The Nile carried silt downstream. Who can tell me what silt is?"

"Rocks?" Guesses Carter. He looks sideways at me. "Pop rocks?"

"Not exactly," says Mrs. Bowen. I think it's the first time Carter has ever answered wrong, but he doesn't seem to care.

After class, I walk to my locker, where Mia is standing. "Carter Griffin almost bumped into me," she says dreamily.

"He's so annoying," I tell her.

"What? You don't think he's cute?"

I slam my locker closed. "Nope."

She looks at me with wide eyes. "You're probably the only girl at Treasure Valley Middle who doesn't."

Ugh.

I go home after school, open my Lists Notebook, and add to the first page.

Practical Rules for Life

#6 Avoid doing more than two summersaults in public.

I turn to my *Becoming Netopedia Notable* list and scribble off *Gymnastics*. I scribble so hard it makes a small hole in the paper.

CHAPTER 13

Day 13. Bacon

My thighs and back still ache when I wake up on Saturday morning. I rush to the computer to check symptoms of deadly diseases that start with back pain.

"I have *cauda equina syndrome*," I announce to GC as I walk into the kitchen. It smells how a kitchen should smell: toasty and bacony.

Mom hates the smell of bacon. She says that it sticks to your hair and clothes and for the entire day everyone around can smell what you ate for breakfast.

Mom and GC may be mother and daughter, but they are nothing alike. GC grew up in the South and moved to Minnesota after she married my Grandpa. She says that you can take a girl out of the South but you can never take the South out of the girl. Mom, on the other hand, is pure

Minnesota: cold and crisp. GC is sunshine, lemons, bacon, and muffins. Mom is broccoli and bleach.

"Darlin' I don't know what you've got," says GC. "But bacon might cure it."

"I doubt it. I'll be paralyzed soon," I tell her. "But at least I won't be hungry." I pile bacon on a paper towel to take into the bathroom. I lay it on the counter while I soak in the bath, and every once in a while I reach over to break off a little piece. GC could be right. Bacon and a bath might actually cure cauda equina syndrome.

My hair is wrapped in a towel and I'm headed to the kitchen for a bacon refill when I hear Mom whispering to GC. "You realize that she's a hypochondriac, right?"

I know who they're talking about. To confirm it, I walk into the kitchen. GC picks up the dishcloth and scrubs an imaginary spot on the counter. Just as I predicted.

"Hypochondriac? That sounds awful," I say. "Whatever it is, I am sure I have it. Do people die from it?"

GC nods and pats my head. "Yes. Yes, it's fatal."

"Sophie." Mom sighs impatiently. "It means you imagine illnesses."

"What are you saying?" I am shocked that my own mother is so cold, so indifferent to her own daughter's suffering. "You're saying I *imagine* I am sick?"

CHAPTER 14

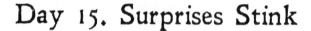

Day 15. Surprises Stink

"I know what the word *hypochondriac* means," I admit to Dr. Williams-the-therapist the following Monday afternoon. His office does not look like the ones from movies. He does not have sofas to lie on or shelves filled with books he's written. Instead, there are bright orange and red beanbags scattered on the floor and framed Dr. Seuss quotes lining the walls. Dr. Williams is a chubby old guy who likes to listen to other people's problems. I don't know why. It seems like a depressing job to me. Maybe listening helps him feel better about his own issues.

"Why did you pretend like you didn't know what it was?" Dr. Williams asks me.

"It was just funner that way," I say.

He nods slowly, and I watch the extra skin from his chin sag toward his chest. "So, you sometimes pretend things, in order to entertain yourself?" he says.

"I guess," I admit. "You have to find humor where you can, right?"

"So, do you pretend to be sick because it's fun? Or do you like the attention?" This guy should not call himself a child psychologist. He definitely does not understand teenagers very well. Or maybe he's an imposter. Maybe *he* is the one who is pretending. That would be just like an adult: to lecture me about something that he does himself.

"I don't *pretend* to be sick," I explain patiently. "I just don't like surprises. Dad's stomach hurt for a while, but he ignored it. And then—bam! Out of nowhere came cancer. I'm not going to be hit with anything like that. I'm going to have plenty of warning."

I hated surprises even before Dad's illness popped up. They give you no warning, so you can't gear up, you can't prepare yourself for the worst possible scenario. Surprises give you no chance to anticipate what you'll say or plan an escape. If you gear up, anticipate the arrival of the end, you're not stupefied when it actually happens.

CHAPTER 15

Day 15 (continued).
Roosters

Trevor is in the van when mom picks me up from my appointment with Dr. Williams. "We're headed to Dad's office," she says in a fake cheery voice.

"Why? Why would we go to Dad's office if he's not there?"

"Because another dentist is taking it over, and we need to clean out Dad's things."

I consider refusing to get out of the van, but it's 100 degrees outside, and as soon as we pull into a parking spot, Mom turns off the engine and takes the key.

Trevor grabs some empty boxes from the back of the minivan. "Can we hurry? I've got places to be."

The receptionist, who is not Ms. Pat (what happened to her?!) escorts us to Dad's office, which is like his den at home: still, dark, waiting.

I don't remember the last time I was in Dad's office, but it surprises me. Not the dark wood desk in the middle of the room, the family photos, or Ollie's drawings plastered on every free inch. I'm surprised by the paintings lining the walls. Painting after painting of roosters, seven of them. They look remarkably similar, although a few of the roosters are black instead of golden brown.

"Dad liked roosters?" I ask Mom, who is also taking them in.

"I don't know. I guess it's been a while since I was here." Mom eyes the roosters suspiciously. "He never mentioned them. They're very… rustic, aren't they?"

We pack up the office and head home. Mom is silent on the drive home and I don't dare say anything out of fear she'll start crying. We stack the boxes and all seven rooster paintings in the garage at home until Mom figures out what to do with it all. "That's enough for today," she says as she heads toward her room. She's probably going to take another shower.

CHAPTER 16

Day 16. Corn Dogs

With gymnastics out, I move on to the best option on my list. "Who is your favorite singer?" I ask my friends at lunch the next day.

"Country? Rap? Pop?" asks Jessie. She's always up on the latest trends. Today she's wearing black-rimmed glasses (though I'm relatively sure she found them at the dollar store), a khaki belted jacket, and gladiator sandals.

I look down at my wrinkled t-shirt with a ketchup stain from those corn dogs I ate a few weeks ago and try to picture myself as a rap star. I don't think it's happening. I am not remotely cool enough and there's no way I can talk fast enough to be a rapper. I can't even pronounce *penicillin* without getting tongue-tied.

I don't own a pair of cowboy boots, so country is out.

"Definitely pop."

"I love Maddie Miller," says Ashley.

I've heard of her, who hasn't? She's only a teenager but her achy, heartbroken songs are on the radio constantly.

"How do you think she got started?" I ask.

"She started playing guitar and singing when she was about eight." Of course Jessie knows Maddie Miller's complete history.

My chances of being a pop star may be a little lower than 10%. I don't know how to sing outside of the shower and I'm not eight. But I have Dad's guitar and I could start practicing immediately. Maybe my first gig can be the school talent show. I get a little queasy thinking about playing in front of the school, but you can't be a singer if you never step out on stage.

CHAPTER 17

Day 16 (continued). Guitars

The house is empty when I get home. I walk through my parents' room and into their closet. My dad's clothes still hang on his side. I bury my face in his shirts and inhale. The smell of laundry soap and his cologne fills me. For a minute he's here again, his strength filling the room.

And then, just as suddenly, he's gone and emptiness takes his place. I swipe at my eyes (stupid things–all they do is leak) and find the guitar in the back of the closet, buried under dirty clothes. I take it out and run my fingers over the strings.

Then I stop to wait for the memories to settle in, like a descending fog.

He played the guitar the way GC kneads bread, with tender but strong fingers coaxing out notes.

Usually, he played old country songs, the kind that belong around a campfire but sometimes he sang silly songs meant to tease the grumpiness out of us. The last time he sang to me, he was sick. He lay on the couch, his head propped on a pillow, his voice weak.

> *Sophie Wofie, the girl of my dreams,*
> *She's not as prickly as she seems.*
> *As pretty and smart as you'll ever see,*
> *Oh Sophie, won't you dance with me?*

I already knew the words, so I'm sure he had sung that to me before. I just can't remember when.

I shake my head to clear my brain and try to remember his voice, clear and strong before cancer stole it. Stupid cancer. It invades and crowds its way into everything. Even memories are not safe from its poison.

I hear voices and the slamming of a door, which means I am not alone anymore. I don't really want to explain why I'm sitting in the middle of a closet with Dad's guitar balanced on my knees. I place it back into the case, close the latches, and tiptoe to my room.

And then I put the guitar back on my knees and stare at it, feeling lost, and then I shake it off. I don't allow myself to feel that way anymore. Practical Rule for Life #1. Break the huge thing into small things.

My LISTS notebook is not in my desk drawer, but I find it under my bed, along with three dirty socks, a Sharpie, and an old box of Dots candy. I pop a green dot in my mouth and open the notebook and turn to my Netopedia list. I skip the scribble hole where gymnastics used to be and add to number three.

> 3a. Steps to be a famous singer.
>   a. Write some songs.
>   b. Practice singing.
>   c. Learn to play guitar.
>   d. Record some music.
>   e. Concerts for my fans.

I take a deep breath and hope for inspiration. While I wait, I strum the guitar. Most of Maddie Miller's songs are about love found and then lost. I haven't found or lost love yet and I'm only twelve, but that's almost a teenager. And I've already seen plenty of teenage boy drama.

Our love has only just begun.
But you are my sunscreen in the burning sun.

I sit back, impressed with myself. It sounds a little like a second-grade valentine, but it's not bad for a first try. Then I imagine myself on stage, singing to thousands of fans screaming my name. But I wouldn't want a boy (especially Carter) to think I have a crush on him. He could think the song is about him. I could toss in a name, just to throw him off, but it has to be the name of a boy I don't know.

It's hard because there are two thousand kids in my school and half of them are boys. That's a lot of names I can't use. I may have to go way back to names from the olden days.

LaRoy, I don't mean to annoy.
Just say the word and you'll be my cowboy.

Not quite right.

Hey there Bill, you're mine until
You get a disease and die on a hill.

Maybe I shouldn't mention a disease in a love song.

My heart thumps when I see you, Larry
You'd be my boyfriend if you weren't so hairy.

Okay. Writing a song is actually harder than I thought.

Maybe I should change the order of my steps. I'll learn to sing first. I can practice on some Maddie Miller songs and then I can concentrate on writing my own.

I blast one by Maddie Miller, belt it out with her, and then I turn off my iPod and try to sing it alone. It sounds...well, not as good as we sounded together. I need more practice.

I'm in the middle of my fourth song when GC knocks on my door. "What are you up to?" she asks.

"Nothing," I say. "Just doing a little voice practice."

"Oh," she says. "Are you feeling sick?"

"I'm alright," I tell her. "Why?"

"You sounded a little...hoarse."

"It's because I am not warmed up yet," I say.

She nods. "It's time for dinner."

CHAPTER 18

Day 18. Lice

I haven't turned in all the assignments I missed, and I have an 81 percent in Social Studies. I think of dumb Carter, who probably has an A, and I'm annoyed. I spend three hours after school on an ancient Greece worksheet until GC calls me for dinner.

When I go downstairs to the kitchen, Trevor's head is in the fridge and Mom is standing at the kitchen counter. She's reading from a bright yellow piece of paper.

"...an outbreak of lice at A Child's World. Please monitor your child and keep him or her home if you notice any sign of lice."

I glance at Ollie, who looks innocent, and remember burying my nose in his hair yesterday. My head itches.

"Ollie has lice?" I ask as casually as I can.

"No," answers Mom. "Someone at his preschool does. He hasn't been there for three weeks, remember?"

"Ooooo lice," says Trevor. He runs his fingers through Ollie's hair and pretends to pick out something. "Delicious," he says, sticking it into his mouth with a grin. "Want a taste, Sophie Wofie?"

I know he's teasing, but the thought makes my head itch.

"Maybe you'd like a taste of this." I shake my fist in his face.

GC steps between us. I give my head a good scratch and go to the sink to wash my hands.

"What's for dinner?" I ask, feeling triumphant that I've handled this lice outbreak so calmly. I want to run upstairs to the shower right now, but I don't want to be dramatic or give Trevor any more ammunition.

We sit at the kitchen table to eat pepperoni pizza. Mom asks Trevor and me questions about school. Trevor grunts; I answer.

"I'm glad you two have adjusted so well," she says. "It's time for the rest of this family to follow your lead. On Monday I'm going back to work and Ollie's going back to preschool."

"Ollie's going back to preschool *now*? With a lice outbreak?" My head itches again.

"Sophie." Mom sighs impatiently. "It's time. And there are not lice at Ollie's preschool anymore."

Like I believe that. I haven't studied lice, at least not yet, but I am pretty sure they live long lives and lurk in all sorts of hidden nooks. As soon as I can, I escape to my room. I need to wash my hair.

CHAPTER 19

Day 23. More Roosters

Apparently, all seventh graders must take CCA – College and Career Awareness, which I think is a waste of time. Last week Mr. Morales assigned us to stand up in class and talk about our parents' careers. I decide to skip dentistry and talk about nursing. There's only so much you can say about teeth. We go alphabetically, A-E on Monday, F-J on Tuesday. I'm on Wednesday, which gives me plenty of time to prepare.

It's Carter's turn on Tuesday. He stands with a large frame covered with a brown tablecloth. "My dad's not around," he says. "But my mom is an artist."

He unveils the frame with a swoosh, and I stare...at a painting of a rooster, which looks very familiar.

"She specializes in roosters," he says, proudly, and bows when the class claps.

I forget to clap because I'm so shocked. Another rooster painting? I thought all of the rooster paintings in the entire world were probably stacked in our garage.

I find him after class. "Hey, Carter. Do you know my dad?"

He lifts his book off his desk. "Pop Rock!"

My mind races to think of some way to tease him. "Hello...Egypt."

It's probably the dumbest thing anyone has ever said, but he laughs like it's the funniest. I don't have time for his dumb names. "Do you know my dad?"

"I don't think so. Why would I know him?" he says as he dashes out of CCA. We only have five minutes between classes, and the classroom is already empty.

"He's a dentist," I call to the back of his head. "Was. He was a dentist."

He doesn't look back. I decide, once again, that he's annoying. And that I don't even care about his stupid roosters.

CHAPTER 20

Day 24. Banana Laffy Taffys

Ollie dresses as Darth Vader for Halloween. The kid is obsessed with bad guys, and according to Ollie, Darth Vader is the worst bad guy there is. When Ollie bursts through my door on Halloween morning, he's breathing like Darth Vader. He reaches toward me and slowly clenches his fingers.

We've played this game before and I know what to do. I grab my neck and gasp for air. He giggles as I fall to the floor. I'm not sure that Ollie pretending to kill people is healthy, and I make a mental note to consult GC. Ollie might need to talk to Dr. Williams-the-therapist.

I haven't thought about my costume since I ate lunch with the popular girls a couple of weeks ago. I'm sure my friends are dressing up, but I missed that discussion, and dressing like them seems wrong anyway. I feel different from them, like I don't quite fit in anymore.

It takes some work, but by the end of the day I've come up with my best costume yet. When I get home from school, I rummage through the costume bin and pull out a wig and a white lab coat.

I put the wig on the top of the globe in the office and trim, smash, comb and gel the hair until it looks right. Then I swipe eyeliner from Mom's makeup stash and draw a mustache and beard on my face.

"Let me guess," GC says when I walk into the kitchen in my costume. "You are...wow, that's a tough one. Christopher Columbus?"

"I am Louis Pasteur, the father of germ killing. He is sort of my hero."

"Of course," she says. "And is Louis Pasteur ready to take Darth Vader trick or treating?"

"I am going with my friends," I tell her. "I have plans with Ashley, Mia, and Jessie."

"That's great," she says. "Can you take Ollie to a couple of houses first? Your mom is at work, and I'm fixin' to hand out homemade donuts."

I sigh. It's a lot of work to have a grandmother who wants to feed all of Arizona. "I guess. Come on Ollie."

But Ollie is not satisfied with a few houses. At the first house, he decides he can't quit until he has filled up his entire pillowcase, preferably with tiny boxes of Dots. Thirty-nine houses later, my friends are long gone.

I spend the rest of the night serving GC's donuts to trick-or-treaters and their parents. Mostly their parents, who gobble donuts faster than the kids. By nine o'clock, GC is out of dough and I'm forced to raid Ollie's pillowcase. He says it's alright, as long as I don't give away his Dots.

At 9:15, when only banana flavored Laffy Taffys are left in the bowl, I open the door to three teenagers. The baseball player has black goop smeared under his eyes, and I'm suddenly happy that we're out of good candy. He doesn't deserve Snickers or Dots.

He opens his bag and holds it out.

"Aren't you supposed to say 'Trick or Treat'?" I remind him.

"Yep. I'd prefer a Treat."

"This is all we have left, Carter," I say, dropping five Laffy Taffys in his bag.

"Pop Rock?" He squints at me. "Is that you?"

"Nope," I tell him. "I'm Louis Pasteur."

"The germ-killing dude?"

I stare. "You know him?"

His friends interrupt from halfway down the sidewalk. "See ya, Smelly Pasture. Come on Carter! We've got to finish this block."

"Ok. See you at school, Sophie."

Sophie. He called me Sophie.

CHAPTER 21

Day 30. Walruses

By the first week of November, I'm back in the school groove like I was never even gone. Most of all, I'm anxious to get started with my plan. On Tuesday, I breeze through the day and ride the bus home. Luckily, I come home to an empty house and I can practice singing as loudly as I want. I need to warm up before anyone comes home.

I'm in the middle of a song when I hear Trevor howling outside my bedroom door. I yank it open. He's laughing so hard his face is red. Even worse, he's got a group of friends behind him and they're laughing too.

"You sound like a dead walrus," he says.

"A dead walrus can't sing," I yell at him. "It's dead."

I throw a shoe at his head to emphasize my point. Unfortunately, it hits the wall instead of his pimply nose. He and his friends thump down the stairs, singing.

One pimple nose thumps another. "You're actually worse than Sophie."

"Not even possible," says the first.

They'll be sorry. They're laughing now but they'll be eating their words when I am a famous singer. I'll write some song called 'Who's The Loser Now?' and tell the world my brother and his friends inspired it. And I will never give them free concert tickets. They'll have to stand in line to buy them with the rest of my fans.

I'm so mad I can't even finish warming up so I go downstairs to help GC. She's trying to restore the kitchen to its pre-Trevor state.

"What was Trevor doing here?" I asked her. "He's never home. Why today?"

"I don't know," she says. "But I'm glad he brought friends here. It's good for him to be home."

"Good for who?" I grumble.

"Whom." She corrects me automatically. She looks at me and softens. "Come here, sweetie." She pulls me to a kitchen chair and sits down next to me. Her knees touch mine. I relax a little as the scent of lemons drifts toward me. "What is going on with you? Why are you suddenly...singing?"

"No reason," I say. "Except I may sing at the school talent show."

I've made a big announcement and I sort of expect GC to jump up and cheer or something. After all, this is what she wants, right? She wants me to get back to normal. I think that's what everyone is sort of impatiently waiting for: me, Mom, and Ollie to act like we are over it. I don't include Trevor in this list because he already acts like it didn't affect him.

GC doesn't cheer. "When is the talent show?" she asks instead.

"I'm not sure. Maybe this spring?"

"Well then," she reaches over and pats my hand. "We'll have time to get you some voice lessons."

"Voice lessons?" I say, offended. "I don't need voice lessons. Maybe guitar, but not voice. You can't just *learn* to sing. Professionals have natural talent."

"Professionals?" She freezes. I hate it when she does that. It throws me off my game.

"I thought we were talking about the school talent show."

"Well, that's just the beginning of my career," I admit.

"Oh sweetie," she says again, shaking her head. "I'm glad you have dreams. Let's get you some voice lessons and start with the talent show."

"GC," I start, trying to be patient. "I am not *dreaming*. I am *planning*."

"And I am glad," she says. "But it doesn't hurt to plan a few lessons."

"I'll consider it," I tell her. "When you tell me how you're famous. Were you a bank robber? "

She laughs. "No, darlin. That would make me *in*famous, and I'm no criminal."

"GC, I'm not giving up that easy."

"I did some things a long time ago but they don't matter now. What matters is all of you. My legacy is my family."

I tell her that sounds like a greeting card, but she clams up. Maybe she was a spy who refused to give up her secrets.

After dinner, I go back to my room and try my best to sound like Maddie Miller. When Mom comes up to say goodnight, she sits on my bed and I groan silently because it's a signal that she wants to talk. I don't have time for emotional chitter-chatter.

"Grandma says you want to take voice lessons," she begins.

"Maybe." I am not committing to anything.

"I think it's great that you have a new interest," she says. "It's a step in the healing process."

I guess I won't mention that it's not healing at all. It is actually preparing for the end, which is inevitable.

CHAPTER 22

Day 33. Screeching

On Friday morning, I am rudely awakened by a horrific screeching sound. It sounds like one of Trevor's friends singing, only worse. And it doesn't stop. I throw off my covers and follow the sound. I push aside a little (ok a bunch) of junk, crawl under the bed and find Trevor's cell phone. As I reach for it, I recognize the song.

It's me. It's actually me singing. I sound horrible, a little like... a dying walrus. I fumble around to silence the phone and open my bedroom door to find Trevor, the fat walrus himself. He's doubled over with laughter. I kick him aside and go to look for GC.

She's in the kitchen, as I expected.

"Do you know who this is?" I ask her. I press *play* and watch her face. GC's not very good at covering up her feelings about things.

She winces a little. "It's you, Sophie. Don't you recognize yourself singing?"

I let my shoulders droop. "I am worse than I thought."

GC squeezes my shoulders. "You just need a little training. And maybe some practice."

"No. Remember what I said yesterday? If someone is not born with talent, her career is over. My career is over, Grandma. Before it even started."

"Are you trying to find a career?" She looks puzzled.

I sit down at the kitchen table. Where is the comfort food when I need it? "Maybe."

"Honey." She pulls a chair out and sits down next to me. "You are beautiful, smart, and funny. You have lots of talents. Maybe singing is just not one of them."

"Thanks a lot," I tell her. "What's for breakfast?"

While she piles my plate with scrambled eggs and hash browns, I pull out Trevor's phone, delete his fantasy football app and download a beauty shop game. Then I turn on the parental controls. He won't be downloading any more apps, surfing the internet, or listening to music that is not G-rated for a really long time. Take that, walrus-head.

From there, my day goes downhill. It is Friday, which unofficially means that teachers are not supposed to assign homework. Mrs. Pringle ignores that rule and assigns a five paragraph argumentative essay on why teachers should not give students homework.

"Do you think she even catches the irony of that?" I ask Mia at lunch.

"Irony?" she asks. Mia is not the best at vocabulary.

To make matters worse, the bags of Cheetos are gone by the time I go through the lunch line and I feel a cold coming on. Or maybe something worse, like pneumonia.

I hand my brownie to Mia and munch an apple slice.

"Are you going to the high school football game tonight?" she asks as she takes a bite of my brownie.

Now that my singing career has been terminated, I'm left without a to-do list, and I've read all the books scattered across the floor of my bedroom.

"Maybe I will," I say. This time I actually mean it.

CHAPTER 23

Day 33 (continued). Old Spice

After school, I go to the kitchen for a cookie. I hear Mom, so I walk to her room to say hey.

"Hey," I say.

Clothes still on hangers are scattered across her bed. "Hi Sophie," she calls from the closet.

"What are you doing?" I ask.

"Organizing." She drops another bunch of clothes on the bed and turns away quickly, but not before I notice that her nose is red.

I sit on the bed and examine the clothes. "These are Dad's," I point out. "What are you doing with them?"

"Donating them." She refuses to look at me.

"What?" It takes a minute for me to understand, but as it dawns on me, my eyes fill, and my chin quivers. "You are giving away Dad's clothes?"

"I have to, Sophie."

"So you can stare at an empty closet instead of Dad's clothes?"

When I was seven or eight my friends and I had tea parties in the swimming pool. We'd sink to the bottom and pretend to drink cups of tea while having a conversation. The challenge was to figure out what the others were saying because their words were enveloped in bubbles of garble.

I feel like that now; like Mom is underwater and I can't understand what she is telling me. My brain is moving in slow motion.

"I can't walk into the closet and see his things and know that he will never walk through the door again. For my sanity, I have to remove the signs of him from my everyday life," she says.

Did she just say she had to remove him? I bury my face in his shirts and wonder if this is what is meant by *moving on*. If so, I want no part of it. "You can't give them away. I need them." I wrap my arms around the pile and clutch it to my chest. If she wants to 'remove him' she'll have to go through me first.

She takes a pair of pants from a hanger. "How about if you pick out two things you'd like to keep?"

"Two?" My voice cracks dangerously. "I'm supposed to remember him with two measly shirts?"

She nods. She is heartless.

This conversation is going nowhere. If I push it, I may cry. Or worse, Mom will. Defeated, I pick up shirts one by one and sniff each. I want the ones that smell most like him.

I smell my way through polo and t-shirts but decide that they are too clean. Laundry detergent has washed his smell away. I wander into the closet, looking for something that would not be freshly washed. Deep on the back of a shelf, I find the Arizona Cardinals sweatshirt. Dad wore it sometimes on game days, but I think he wore it mostly when he wanted to tease Mom. She hated it.

It has holes in the sleeves but it's soft and warm. I roll it into a ball and tuck it under my arm. I don't want her to change her mind when she sees what I've chosen. Next, I grab his fishing vest. I am not sure what use a fishing vest has, especially now, but when I see it I remember him standing at the edge of the water putting a worm on my hook or untangling my line.

I take his sweatshirt and vest into the kitchen and try to cram them into a zip-top bag but neither will fit so I settle for a white garbage bag. I need to preserve the smell as long as possible.

Smell. It occurs to me suddenly that his scent is actually bottled. I carry the bag back into the bedroom, avoid the closet where Mom's sniffling, and head for the bathroom.

"Mom?" I call. "Can I have Dad's cologne?"

I almost think that she didn't hear me because she doesn't answer right away. "Don't you think we should give it to Trevor? He can probably use it."

I make a face. Stinky Trevor smelling like Dad? No way. I start opening drawers in my parents' bathroom until I see three bottles of cologne and a stick of red Old Spice deodorant. Two of the bottles are almost full, one has a few drops at the bottom. I take the lid from the empty bottle and sniff. I am a genius. It's him, all bottled up.

I smell the other two and frown. They stink, and Trevor can have them. He can cover his stinkiness with their stink.

Dad's toothbrush is in the top drawer and I pick it up for examination. I am surprised that his toothbrush looks like mine. The bristles are mashed down and there are tooth marks on the back. I open the drawer on Mom's side. It's clean and organized; her toothbrush looks new. It is another sign of what I already knew. I am much more like my Dad than my Mom.

My mom has gone from sniffling to outright crying, and I can't listen. It makes my throat ache.

"I think I'll go to the high school football game tonight," I call to her from the bathroom. "I'm going with Ashley and Jessie."

"Alright," she sniffles after a few seconds. I'm not sure she understood, but I don't think it matters. She will barely notice I am gone.

I stuff the loot under my bed and call Ashley.

CHAPTER 24

Day 33 (continued again). Germy Hands

I have not been to many football games, but Ashley and Jessie have. They tell me that seventh-grade girls don't go to games to actually watch football. They go to hang out with friends and catch glimpses of middle school boys.

"Come on," Mia pulls at me. "I saw Carter Griffin."

"You want to talk to Carter Griffin?"

"Don't you think he's cute?"

I think of his sandy brown hair and the freckles dotting his nose and then I force that thought from my mind. "Not at all. He's a know it all. He answers every question in class."

Mia glances at me like I'm dumb. "So do you, Sophie."

"Really?" I search for another reason she shouldn't like him. "He teases. And he hangs out with those dumb football players."

"What's wrong with them?" says Ashley, before we run into a group.

Carter is not among them, and Mia loses interest quickly. "We're going to the stands to watch the football game," she tells Ashley, who is flirting with Damian Gonzales. I can't believe she likes him. The memory of Damian picking his nose in second grade will stay in my mind forever. I should warn Ashley. *Imagine holding those germy hands.*

We find seats on the fifth row and squint to see the game.

"Hey Sophie," Carter calls to me as he walks past. I wave, but only because he didn't call me Pop Rock.

"You know him? He knows your name?" Mia accuses.

I shrug. "He's in a couple of my classes."

The crowd jumps to its feet and roars.

Football really is a dumb sport. People run around chasing a ball and slamming each other against the ground. The chances of a person getting smashed into a thousand little pieces seem very high. But there's something about the lights and cheers that draws me in. People are cheering. The players are important and *notable*.

The kicker trots onto the field. He is thin and tall, and he looks out of place, like he belongs on a soccer field instead of a foot... *A soccer field.* I am a soccer player. I may not be the greatest, but I am much more of a soccer player than a gymnast.

Football looks even easier than soccer. The ball is bigger and someone actually holds it for the kicker. Anyone could score a goal in soccer if someone held the ball in place right in front of the goal.

I could be a professional football kicker. If that's not notable, I don't know what is. I call GC to ask her to come pick me up right away. I've got some research to do.

Becoming Netopedia Notable

#4 Football.

The list is changing fast.

CHAPTER 25

Day 33 (even longer). Chocolate Shakes

Although it's dark outside, I decide to start practicing immediately. I walk into the garage in search of a football. I flip on the fluorescent lights and wait for them to hum to life. The smell of the garage drifts toward me: gasoline mixed with decaying grass, but I like it somehow. It's comfortingly normal, the first thing that has obeyed my instructions to the universe and stayed the same. I wander past the weedwhacker and bikes to the plastic ball bin in the corner. I paw through the bin and pull out a cracked baseball helmet, a street hockey stick, the shriveled core of an apple, three rollerblades, and a basketball. I pick up the basketball and feel it sag in my hands.

"Grandma!" My voice echoes through the laundry room as the garage door slams behind me. "Where is our football?"

I walk into the kitchen, where Grandma and Ollie sit at the kitchen table lining up dominoes. GC's hand hovers above a teetering line. "You're looking for a *football?*" she asks, staring at me as if I just asked her if I could eat Trevor's stinky socks.

"Yep." I try to sound casual. "I'm thinking of trying out for the football team."

"Football?" she echoes faintly.

I shift my feet. I don't have time to hang around and wait until she understands. "Yeah. Have you seen our football?"

"Hmmm. I don't believe I've seen a football. But I saw your soccer ball in the back seat of your Dad's car."

Dad's car is still in the garage. I just walked past it and it didn't even occur to me that it didn't belong there anymore. I guess in her quest to get rid of all things Dad, Mom hasn't worked her way to the garage.

She's probably still sitting cross-legged on the floor of his closet. Worse yet, she's probably crying. I shake my head to clear the image. I hate it when she cries. I hate it when bad things happen and I have no power to change them. The most horrible feeling in the world is helplessness, and the only way out of it is pretending the problem doesn't exist.

I walk into the garage where Dad's black Honda sits next to the minivan. I see my soccer ball on the floor of Dad's car but I can't make myself open the door. The car remembers him and our life before. The backseat windows are smeared with Ollie's fingerprints, the leather seats are scuffed. I see a dent on the front bumper from the time Dad taught Trevor to parallel park. I imagine there are old McDonald's receipts shoved in his door and napkins lying on the floor from the last time he took me to get a chocolate shake and I spilled it.

The inside of the car is PC. Pre-cancer. He stopped driving it six months ago when he got sick. After that Mom drove her minivan to Dad's doctor appointments and hospital visits. In the last few weeks, the minivan came in handy because he could lie down in the back. He got so weak even the seat belt couldn't hold him up.

Bad memories splatter the minivan like mud. Dad's car may be dirty and dented, but it's still PC.

I back away. I'm afraid if I open the door, a memory will escape into the air and evaporate. The soccer ball can stay where it belongs. I need a football anyway.

CHAPTER 26

Day 34. Blueberry Muffins

When I wake up I swallow and wait to feel pain. It doesn't come so I listen for creaks in my knees and rumbling of my stomach. It's strange, and a little disappointing that not even my head hurts this morning. And then I remember that today is Saturday and that I have plans. I leap out of bed and run to the kitchen where I see GC sitting at the kitchen table with the newspaper.

"Good morning, sweet Grandma." I wrap my arms around her shoulders. I almost tip over her bottle of Dr. Pepper but she catches it in time.

"Who are you?"

I laugh. "What is for breakfast?"

She sits her soda down and studies me. "How are you feeling?"

"Like a million bucks." It's a lie; I have never felt like a million bucks, but I am enjoying the look on her face. I like to surprise her.

"Are there any blueberry muffins left?"

"One left." She hands me the muffin and Section E. "Here are your obituaries."

"I don't need those today. Who reads a newspaper anymore anyway?"

"Ok, pumpkin. What's going on?" Her eyes crinkle with worry as she looks at me.

It's wrong to make her worry, but I can't help but soak it up a little. It makes me feel better to know that she cares.

"I am ok, GC. Want to practice kicking a football today?"

"Only if you spill the beans," she says. "I know you're up to something. Spit it out; fess up."

I sigh. "I told you. I'm going to be a football player."

"But..." She looks me up and down. "Won't you get hurt?"

I can't help but feel cheerful. "That's the beauty of it, GC. I'll be the *kicker*. They just make points, they don't get tackled. Kickers get all the glory but none of the guts." I think that's a saying I heard somewhere. I'm proud of myself for remembering it because it really fits in this situation.

Mom walks into the kitchen dressed in her scrubs. Her keys jingle as they dangle from her fingers.

"Mama!" cries Ollie. He runs to her.

She hugs him and eyes GC and me. "What have you guys been up to?"

"Nothing," I say quickly, mentally instructing GC not to volunteer information.

GC avoids my eyes. "Sophie was just fixin' to play some football."

"Great," Mom says as if she didn't hear. She peels Ollie from her leg, pecks my cheek, and turns to GC. "Thanks, Mom."

I wait until the door shuts and then I explode. "Charlotte Taylor! Can you not keep a secret?"

"Now darlin," she says. "Don't you go pitchin' a hissy fit. Your mom didn't even notice what I said."

I can't disagree. "Maybe," I allow. "Will you come to the park and help me? I need someone to hold the football so I can kick it."

GC lifts Ollie onto the countertop. "Not now, hon. I'm as busy as a one-legged cat in a sandbox," she says.

"Please, Grandma. You are crucial to my career!"

She stops and stares at me, lifting one eyebrow. "Career? What career?"

Darn. I almost spilled the beans, as GC would say. I try to redeem myself with a partial lie. "I...didn't mean career as in grown-up *career*. I meant my sports-playing days. You are the key to my teenage happiness."

"I thought singin' in the school talent show was the key to your teenage happiness."

I sigh. "That was last week, GC. I've moved on from singing. You need to keep up."

"I can't keep up with you. You change your mind more often than your underwear."

"That's not true. I am a very clean person."

She winks at me. "I know you are, pumpkin. I was just teasing."

"Well," I say. "Now you owe me. You can make it up by holding the football."

I've got her. We head to River Park six blocks from our house and walk to the open field. I hand GC the ball and back up.

I run but tap the ball half-heartedly. GC is holding the ball, and I'm nervous I'll kick her. My ball skips twice and skids to a stop a couple of feet away.

Ollie boos.

"That all you got?" GC says. "Cause that was weak."

"Oh yeah? Let's see you do better."

GC nods like it's an easy challenge. She ties her tennis shoes, picks up a stick, and pokes it in the grass to mark where my ball landed. She winks at Ollie and throws me the football.

I kneel down and hold the top with my forefinger. I'm a little nervous that she's going to hurt herself. It's not easy to kick a football.

GC backs up, runs toward the ball, and kicks. It sails over the marking stick and lands at the edge of the grass leading to the playground.

The sideline audience cheers, and the audience number has definitely increased. I look to the sideline, where Ollie is sitting with... Carter Griffin and Lilly, from my gymnastics class.

What is he *doing here?* I mutter to myself and decide to ignore him. He picks up the ball and throws it to GC, who catches it like she's a superstar receiver.

"GC!" I yell. "Where'd you learn to play football?"

She laughs. "Athletic genes. I handed them down to you, Sophie. You just have to dig them out."

I laugh as she hugs me. "GC, you could be famous. *Football star Grandma kicks the winning goal.*"

"No," she says, "I'm too busy training Ollie to line up dominoes and watching *The Price is Right*. I'll let you be the star."

She kneels in the grass. She may be a football star, but it takes her a minute to get down. And I'm not sure she'll make it back up. She nudges the nose into the grass and holds the top with her fingertip.

"Come on, sunshine. Let's see what you've got."

I think of my last kick puttering across the lawn. I've got an audience and this can't sputter. I visualize the ball soaring into the air, sailing through the air.

Soar! I repeat to myself as I run toward it with all my might. I close my eyes and lift my foot...

...and I miss. I completely miss the ball, and the force of the kick sends me flying onto my back.

I lay for a minute with my eyes closed, hoping to be magically transported to any other place, any other time. I don't, and when I open my eyes, GC, Ollie, and Carter encircle me, concerned.

"Like that?" I croak.

Carter laughs and offers me his hand. "You just need a little practice."

"Yes, she does. Will you coach her?" says GC, heading to the sideline with Ollie and Lilly.

"No!" I say. "He can't. He's...busy."

She winks at me. "She's a little headstrong," she says to Carter.

Carter laughs. "Come on, Pop Rocks." He holds out his hand to pull me up.

I sigh, defeated.

"I'm not really a kicker," he explains as he kneels to hold the football. "But I think you need to keep your eyes on the ball."

I back up and glare at the ball, that dumb thing that refuses to fly, and then I back up, run, and tap at it half-heartedly.

"Come on," GC says to the kids. "Let's go to the playground. This is gonna take a while."

"Ok," says Carter. "At least you got your foot on it. This time when you run, plant your left foot at this spot and kick with your right."

I know how to do this; I've been playing soccer since I was five. I don't know why my brain refuses to remember that.

"This may not be my sport," I tell him after I've kicked (well, kicked is an optimistic word) eleven balls.

He plops down on the grass. "Why are you trying to play football?"

I don't really want to tell him about my quest for fame. It's sort of embarrassing.

"I just wanted to try something new."

"That's cool."

"What are you doing here, anyway?"

He glances toward the playground like he's just remembered he brought someone. "I promised Lilly that I'd practice soccer with her."

He gets up. "I should probably go get her."

"Yeah. I'm an ok soccer player. Want to play a game?"

Ollie and I line up against Carter and Lilly and argue over GC.

"Clearly, it's the Murphys against the Griffins," I argue. "GC's ours."

"I'm not a Murphy," GC reminds me. "I'll sit on this bench and watch. Besides a sudoku puzzle is calling my name,"

Ollie and I win by 2, but only because we slightly cheat.

CHAPTER 27

Day 34 (continued). Broken Eggs

"Football is not my sport either," I inform GC when we get home.

"What? I thought you had fun." GC pours herself a glass of lemonade. I reach for it, and she slides it over. "Besides, Murphys don't quit."

"They don't quit *trying*," I clarify. "Sometimes it takes a few experiments, and maybe a few explosions, to figure out what a person's really good at."

She nods. "Sometimes you have to break a few eggs to make an omelet."

"Exactly. And I'd rather break eggs than legs."

GC laughs. "That's a pretty good line."

It is, I decide, and I add it to my Practical Rules.

7. Break eggs, not legs.

CHAPTER 28

Day 36. Vampires

I'm sort of nervous to see Carter on Monday, though I can't really explain why. After successfully avoiding him all day, I almost walk straight into him on my way out of the school. My head was in a book, but he shares half of the blame. He's standing in the middle of the sidewalk.

"Pop Rock!"

"Hey." I walk faster

He catches up to me. "Hey, Sophie. Is your Dad Dr. Murphy? The dentist?"

I stop. "Yeah."

"Dr. Murphy was my dentist," he says. "He was a nice guy. I'm really sorry that he died."

"Thanks," I say.

He chuckles. "We had a dentist appointment last Halloween. Dr. Murphy was dressed up like a vampire. He had a cape, slicked back hair, and fangs. Lilly freaked out when she laid back in the chair and he stood above her with his fangs sticking out."

"My mom told him not to wear that vampire costume, but he refused to take it off." I laugh, remembering. "Hey. Did you know that my dad has some of your mom's paintings?"

He looks at me dubiously. "Are you sure? She hasn't even sold any."

The roosters in my garage look just like the rooster he showed the class, but I haven't gotten close enough to notice the signature on the painting. "Maybe I'm thinking of another rooster artist."

"So how's your football career?" he says.

I laugh. "I'm not cut out to be a professional kicker. Or a gymnast. Or a tight rope walker."

I hear a honk. GC is waving at me from the minivan. "I've got to go."

CHAPTER 29

Day 38. Failure

I'm serious about what I told Carter. I'm striking out on everything. My quest for a Netopedia listing has stalled. I pull out The List, stare at it and add the likelihood of success.

Becoming Netopedia Notable
  1. *Politician / 0%*
  2. *Hockey player / 0%*
  3. *Singer*

I think back to the recording and wince. Is it possible to have less than zero percent?

  4. ~~*Gymnast*~~
  5. *Football player.*

Football fields are very long and kicking a ball through some poles is not as easy as it looks. It will take a long, long time before I'd be any good at kicking a stupid football. It could take years. I picture myself at GC's age, finally kicking the ball across the field, finally getting a Netopedia mention, and then I scribble out football.

That's four, well five broken eggs and I still don't have an omelet. I may be out of eggs because everything that occurs to me has already been done.

I open the computer to check.

6. *Make the biggest wad of chewed gum.*

Even if I am able to ignore the germs, which is unlikely, it's been done.

7. *Most t-shirts worn at the same time.*

Also done. That accomplishment alone is proof that someone has thought of every idea that ever existed.

8. *Grow the longest fingernails in the world.*

Yuck. I can't do that. Just imagine all the germs lurking under six-inch nails.

I'm out of ideas. And I'm a failure. A nobody.

And I'll probably die that way.

CHAPTER 30

Day 40. Stomping

On Friday, we pull into the driveway and the garage door rolls open. My stomach drops. The garage is empty.

"*Where is Dad's car?*"

"Your mom told Trevor he could start driving it."

"WHAT?"

"There's no sense in letting a car sit in a garage. Trevor needed transportation."

I close my eyes, take a deep breath, and hold it in my chest, the way the therapist taught me.

"Trevor can't just take Dad's things. He can't just *drive Dad's car.* He'll mess it up and stink it up and wreck everything."

How does Trevor think that he has the right to drive it? Trevor doesn't care about Dad or the fact that he is gone. I slam the door of the minivan and stand on the oil stains and tire marks on the floor of the garage. The roosters stare at me with their beady eyes and I want to kick them. Why do we still have those stupid paintings, anyway? We give away his clothes and his cologne, we corrupt his car but we save the roosters?

I stomp outside and toss them in the trash can, slam them on top of the grass clippings. I stew and rage at Trevor for a while, and then I go back out to lift the roosters out of their pit and place them gently back in their corner in the garage.

I don't know why Dad kept them, but if he thought they were important, I do too.

For the next few days, I wander around aimlessly until GC pronounces me either certifiably sick or depressed. "I am both, actually," I tell her.

She tells me to drink a Dr. Pepper and watch an episode of The Price is Right. I doubt this remedy even comes close to the bacon and bath solution, but she insists. "It works eighty-eight percent of the time," she says.

I'm in the twelve percent. Even GC's best remedy doesn't help.

"I'm worried about her," I hear GC whisper to Mom in the kitchen late one night when I get out of bed for a drink of water. "She looked like she was excited about a few things, but now...she no longer has an interest in anything. Not her friends, not school."

Mom sighs. "I know. I think she needs time. We've got to be patient with her."

Silence. I start to tiptoe back to my room but stop when I hear GC's voice. "I think it's time for me to go back to Minnesota. Let you all have time to be alone."

I breathe in so sharply I'm sure they have heard me. GC leaving? Is it possible for things to get any worse?

"Please wait," I hear Mom say. I sink to the floor in the dark hallway. It's uncomfortable and cold, but I refuse to miss any of this conversation.

"Will you stay through the holidays?" Mom says. "I have a feeling they're going to be rough."

GC doesn't answer for a little while. In my mind I see her take a sip of soda and think. "If you still need me, I'll stay," she says at last.

Relieved, I creep back to bed and lay under my covers shivering at the thought of GC leaving.

Practical Rules for Life
    8. GC makes everything better.

CHAPTER 31

Day 43. Apple Pie

Two days before the Thanksgiving break, Mrs. Pringle makes an announcement in Language Arts.

"I expect you all to compete in this year's Impressions Contest. The theme is 'Wonders of Nature'. You may write an essay, story, or poem, draw, or take a photo. Express your creativity. You will be graded and judged accordingly."

We collectively groan. It's nice of the PTA to have contests, but it changes the game when teachers make it mandatory. Basically, it's no longer fun; not that writing an essay ever was.

I consider my options. Maybe I should avoid writing a song. My poetry skills are not that hot either. I'll probably write an essay, boring as it sounds.

I go home to pies. Five of them, sitting on the counter, golden brown, calling for me to taste them. I head toward them with a plate and a fork, but GC bats me away. "You'll have to wait for Thanksgiving," she says.

"That long?" I whine. "I have to smell these things for two days? That's torture, GC."

She points to a pie sitting alone. Its edges are burned a dark brown, filling has escaped and run down the pan. "You can eat that one."

A burned apple pie is better than no apple pie. I cut a thick slice and scrape out the soft inside to shovel inside my mouth. "Why are you making a big deal about Thanksgiving? Don't you know how we do it?"

GC shakes her head absently. She's scribbling a grocery list that looks longer than my last Language Arts essay. GC has never been at our house for Thanksgiving before. She has come for Christmas, but Minnesota is too far from Arizona to come for both holidays. Christmas has always won. I'd better explain our Thanksgiving traditions to her.

"We usually go to a buffet to eat dinner and then we come home and pop a frozen pumpkin pie in the oven. I mean, I'm not knocking your pies because they look amazing. But it looks like a lot of work for one meal."

She shakes her head. "It's time for some new traditions, darlin'. You need to know what a home-cooked Thanksgiving dinner tastes like."

I doubt this is going to work out. Mom tried to roast a turkey once. I guess there's some sort of plastic thingamajigger inside the turkey that you're supposed to take out before you bake it. She forgot to take it out, and we ended up with turkey stuffed with melted plastic. We went out for Thanksgiving that year and every year since then.

GC's a great cook. So if anyone can pull it off, I guess she can. But I'm not so sure a home-cooked Thanksgiving dinner will be a new tradition.

CHAPTER 32

Day 46. Peeling Potatoes

By Thanksgiving morning, I am sure that GC's sole purpose is to torture Ollie and me. We wander around the house sniffing, swiping a taste every few minutes until GC or Mom shoos us out of the kitchen. They allow me to stay only when I volunteer to peel potatoes.

"Where is Trevor?" I ask as I peel. The bigger dots on the potatoes (the eyes, GC calls them) stare at me and I peel them furiously.

"Asleep," says Mom. "But he'll be up for dinner at two. After that, we'll play games. We're going to make new traditions today."

"We are going to play games? All of us? Trevor and Ollie too?" I am not so sure about this plan.

Ollie hears his name and comes running into the kitchen. He's holding a wooden sword in one hand and a cardboard shield in the other. "Got ya!"

he says, poking me with his sword. I clutch my chest and fall off the stool and onto the ground, where I take a deep breath and die dramatically. Ollie giggles. It's good to hear him laugh and I decide I will play with him more. I've heard I have a talent for faking illness or death.

I'm not so sure about games though. When Dad got sick and things didn't look good, Mom tried to force us into "family together time." I am sure that she was disappointed.

The last time we were all together was the first part of September when we took a picnic to the park. I was on board until we parked the car in an empty lot and I opened the car door. The hot air blasted me like I had opened an oven. I mean, if you live in Arizona you understand summers are hot. But we run from air-conditioned car into air-conditioned buildings and hardly feel the heat. Unless you happen to be going on a family picnic.

Dad's muscles had dissolved, leaving his body looking like pointed bones and saggy skin. He could barely shuffle from his bed to the bathroom, let alone walk across the grass to the shade where Mom had laid a blanket. With shaking arms, he lifted himself from the car and stood. He leaned against the car and swayed until Mom and Trevor stretched his arms over their shoulders and dragged him across the grass.

We sat in the shade of a tree, picked at our sandwiches, and guzzled cold sodas until Dad announced that it was time for an inchworm competition. We had to crawl, and the slowest person to the finish line won. Ollie lost, of course. Trevor lost interest fast. Dad and I crept along until Mom announced the end of the competition. It was probably the last time Dad touched grass.

After lunch, Ollie and I ran to the pond to feed the goldfish bread from our sandwiches. We dropped crumbs into the water and watched the fish swarm to eat them. We loved it until a blue heron swooped in uninvited, and dove into the water with an open mouth to trap those defenseless goldfish. Ollie and I screamed at it to leave the fish alone, but it gulped fish and lunged for more.

The stupid heron ignored our screams and kept devouring those fish until its throat glowed orange from the scales inside and the little pond was left mostly empty. I hated that heron.

Now that I'm in the middle of peeling potatoes and have time to think, it occurs to me that herons are like cancer. Both come when you least expect or want them, they gobble up everything in sight and leave only emptiness behind. I hate both cancer and herons.

CHAPTER 33

Day 46 (continued). Pies

No one can resist the smell of roasting turkey, including Trevor. He surfaces at lunchtime, makes himself a sandwich, and taste tests until Mom and GC order him out of the kitchen. Soon the sounds of a football game blare from the family room.

"Trevor," Mom yells, taking rolls out of the oven. "Turn that down!"

The volume of the TV does not change.

"Sophie," she says. "Go tell him to turn that down. We've got enough chaos without that thing blasting."

I walk into the family room. "Mom says to turn it down."

Trevor doesn't move. I walk to the TV and press the button to turn down the volume.

"What are you doing?" Trevor yells. He grabs the remote and turns it back up.

As patient as a kindergarten teacher, I turn it back down.

"Knock it off Walrus Wofie."

I roll my eyes and walk out of the room as the volume increases.

So Mom is sweaty and frustrated by the time dinner is ready. "Trevor! Turn that thing down and come eat!"

Trevor's deaf only until he hears the word 'eat.'

Mom, GC, Ollie, and I are all sitting at the kitchen table when he comes in and plops into an empty chair. He spoons mashed potatoes onto his plate and nods toward the empty spot at the end of the table, where a plate and silverware wait. "Who else is coming?"

"That is Dad's spot," says Mom, her chin trembling.

"Well, that's dumb," says Trevor.

Mom pretends not to hear him. "We're not going to eat until each of us has said something we are thankful for. I will start. I am grateful for each of you. This year has made me realize even more that our loved ones are all we've got."

She dabs her eyes with her napkin and looks to her right, where I happen to be sitting.

"I am thankful for memories," I say, but I don't elaborate.

Trevor is next. We wait for him to swallow. "Food." He shovels another bite in his mouth.

"I feel the same as your mother," GC says. "I am grateful for loved ones. You are all precious to me."

"Dinosaurs," says Ollie next.

"Good one!" Trevor gives Ollie a thumbs up sign and Ollie beams.

"All right then." Mom nods, satisfied at our measly effort. "Let's eat."

It's mostly quiet while we eat, and then Trevor pushes his plate away and starts to get up from the table. Mom eyes him. "Where are you going?"

"Brian's house," he answers. "We're playing football at three."

"No, you're not," Mom says. "You're going to help with dishes and then we're going to play a family game. We are spending the day together. I thought I made myself clear on that."

Trevor glares at her. "What are you talking about? You're saying that I can't go play football with my friends?"

"I am," Mom returns Trevor's glare.

"Well, that's just stupid," he explodes. "This house is lame and so are you and you can't force me to stay here."

"You will," she says evenly, "if you want to drive a car for the next two weeks."

"So if I leave you're going to take my car away?"

"It's not even your car. It's Dad's." I insert.

GC, silent, stares at her plate. Ollie is propped up on his booster seat. He looks back and forth between Mom and Trevor.

"You're not going to tell me what to do." Trevor erupts, his face as red as the inside of the cherry pie on the counter.

"Actually, I am," says Mom. She puts a bite of stuffing into her mouth as if this were a normal conversation during a normal meal.

"I can't believe you." Trevor grabs at his plate and shoves it onto the countertop. It slides and lands in the sink with a crash.

"Did you break that plate?" asks Mom. "Because if you did, you're doing all of the dishes by yourself."

"What?" The redness on Trevor's face deepens.

He walks over to the sink and pulls out half of the plate. He tosses the jagged pieces into the garbage. "You have no right to tell me what to do! You're not in charge of this house."

"I am," she says. "I am the only parent left here."

"You're not here. And you're not a parent anymore. You haven't been a parent since Dad got sick. I wish it would have been you who died. I wish Dad was here instead of you."

She stares at him, motionless, except for the tears running down her cheeks. "I wish that too."

I can't stand it anymore, and I run from the room as he punches a wall. The drywall shudders and then cracks as his fist goes through it.

I curl up on my bed and cry until I fall asleep. When I wake up, my head aches, and I can't think of any disease to blame it on. Trevor's words and Mom's face play in my mind like a bad movie that you hate but you can't stop thinking about. I lie on my bed trying to force them out and suddenly other words come into my mind. Words of an essay.

I get up, rummage through my desk for a pencil and scribble on the back of last week's math homework.

I am not a writer. I've had the same pink flowered diary since I was eight, and I've written in it a total of five times. Three of the entries are Christmas lists.

I have always hated writing homework, but now words flood onto the paper and I can't scribble them fast enough. When the torrent of words finally slows, I've filled three sheets of paper.

I sit back and take a deep breath. Removing words from my brain and limiting them to black and white somehow tames them. In my head, they are large and heavy and threaten to explode from my brain. On paper, they shrink down to look quiet and ordinary, and I am not so afraid of them.

I open my bedroom door and creep toward the kitchen. It's empty, clean, the dishwasher humming. The only signs of a Thanksgiving dinner are the pies on the counter and a new hole in the wall.

I cut myself a big piece of pumpkin pie and watch outside, where GC is playing soccer with Ollie. It looks like he is losing.

CHAPTER 34

Day 51. Beef Stew

My family does not mention what happened on Thanksgiving. We pretend it never happened and pick up with our new normal. A week after Thanksgiving, GC tries to cover up the hole in the kitchen wall. She slaps some gooey white stuff up and even paints over it. It's hardly noticeable, but I can still feel it. I stare at its outline while I eat, and it usually ruins my appetite.

Now that my hopes are dashed and my family is falling apart, I have nothing left in life to look forward to, except maybe GC's blueberry muffins.

A little ray of sunshine comes on the first Friday in December. It arrives routinely. I'm sitting in my first-period class, breathing hard because I barely missed being marked tardy. It is hard to run from the minivan to my math class in

120 seconds, but I did it. I take off my hoodie and partially listen to the announcements.

"Lunch today will be beef stew, salad, and carrot sticks." Gross.

"Remember to bring cans for the food drive. Our annual holiday dance will be held on Friday, December 14 from 1:00 to 3:30 during fifth and sixth period classes. If you choose not to attend the dance, you may study in the library during that time."

The class buzzes and I strain to listen to the conversations around me. Strangely, it seems that only girls care about this news. Emilio and Max, who are sitting behind me, don't seem to care. They're talking about a football game last night as if a major announcement has not just been made.

At lunch over the sickening smell of beef stew, I listen to Ashley and Mia discuss the dance point by point. According to Mia (who is an authority because she has an older sister), the girls talk in groups on one side of the gym; guys on the other. "I heard someone say there will even be a real DJ." Mia is so busy talking she forgets to ask for my brownie, and it stays on her lunch tray where I leave it.

I've seen movies and read books and I know the drill. The princess or heroine always finds her prince at the ball. I know this is not a real ball with big dresses and pumpkin carriages and all that, but I am still excited. It's my first chance at romance, after all. And I know most of the guys in seventh grade like girls with long blonde wavy hair and curvy bodies, but I'm hoping someone is smart enough to see something in common looking girls who are awkward and flat all over but who might be famous for something someday.

CHAPTER 35

Day 54. Roosters

I've decided it's time to get to the bottom of the rooster mystery. I'm striking out with both GC's past and my own quest for fame. It's time to focus on Dad's legacy. It could be connected to roosters, which is rather sad if it's true. I've got to find out.

I've examined the signature on the paintings. The first initial is definitely an A and the last name starts with Gri... and then a squiggly line. I suppose it could say "Griddle" or "Grizzly" but I think it's a pretty safe bet to assume it's signed A Griffin.

Carter's been no help at all, but the clues lead to his mom. I've got to find her, but the thought of tracking Carter makes me feel queasy. It's a little weird.

When GC picks me up after school, I tell her the plan. "I don't want to tell you why; you'll have to trust me. But you've got to follow that bus." I point to Bus 312, which is pulling out of the bus lane onto the street.

GC doesn't even ask. She just follows my instructions. Until twenty-two minutes has passed, and we've stopped behind the bus six times. Then she stops behind the bus, without even bothering to hide the minivan.

"GC!" I scold. "This is a covert operation. I don't want Carter Griffin to think that I'm stalking him."

"Carter?" she explodes. "This whole thing is about some scruffy headed boy? We're traipsing across town to follow some boy?"

"Shhhh," I hold my finger to my lips, even though we're inside the van and there is almost no chance that he'll hear. "It's more than that, GC. It's really important for my *mental well-being*." I throw that last bit in because I know it will persuade her. I know it's a little manipulative, but detectives employ every means at their disposal.

Finally, when we're parked behind a U-Haul truck, I see Carter climb off the bus. "There he is, GC. Stay here with the van, I'll follow him on foot."

I'd worn a camo t-shirt for the occasion, and figured that an ordinary looking girl dodging from tree to tree could hide easier than a white minivan.

Carter walked two blocks south of the bus stop, stops at a small square four-plex, climbs the stairs to the upstairs apartment, and disappears through the door.

"Apartment four," I whisper to myself, and I sneak back to the van.

CHAPTER 36

Day 59. Rico the Rooster

I wait until Wednesday, when I know Carter has football practice, and then I talk GC into driving me again. She's not thrilled, but I promise a rousing game of Five Crowns in exchange.

We park two houses past 413 Casa Verde Street. I'm hardly out of the van when a large yellow dog almost knocks me down. He jumps on me like I'm a slab of prime rib.

"Hey boy," I grab at his collar.

"Boomer!" A lady holding a leash dashes toward us. "I'm so sorry. He's a little crazy today." She brushes reddish-brown hair from her eyes.

"No problem," I say. "He's a cute dog. I'd have a dog like that if my mom would let me." I reach back into the van and pull out the rooster painting I brought.

"Hey," the lady says, noticing my painting. "Where'd you get that?"

I hold it in front of me. "It was hanging in my Dad's office."

"Who's your Dad?"

"Michael Murphy."

"Dr. Murphy? The dentist?"

I nod. "I'm his daughter."

A little girl runs to the dog and wraps her arms around the dog's neck. It licks her face and I shudder. "Hey, Sophie," the girl says.

"Hey, Lilly." I feel slightly less awkward because Lilly and I are friends.

"My dad had seven of these paintings. I'm just trying to figure out why," I say to Carter's mom.

We walk to apartment four and she shoves Boomer through the front door. "Come on in," she says to me. We move through the living room, where Lilly joins an older boy watching TV on a brown sagging sofa.

Carter's mom motions for me to sit down and then laces paint-stained fingers together on the table. "I'm surprised he kept all of them."

"They were hanging in his office."

She nods. "I don't know what I thought he'd do with them, but I had to give him something. Your dad helped me a lot. I offered to pay him, but he knew I'm a single mom and he refused to charge me. I owed him, so I painted Rufus the Rooster. He said that it was a masterpiece and that he'd hang it in his office."

"Rufus." I lift the painting that I brought with me. "Is this Rufus?"

She takes it, examines it. "Nope. This is Rico."

"How do you know?" I ask.

"One knows her art. It's like knowing your babies."

I nod, though I'm as confused as ever. "But there are seven paintings."

She laughs. "My kids eat too much candy."

I look at Rico, the brown rooster I'd leaned against the table leg. His eyes look a little less beady.

The front door slams. "Mom!"

It sounds like Carter, and I want to hide. I'm about to fling myself under the table when he comes into the kitchen. "Sophie? What are you doing here?"

I feel my face burn. "Umm. Hello. I was just here to talk to your mom about these paintings."

His mom opens the fridge, "You know Sophie? Dr. Murphy's daughter?"

"Yeah. We have a class together. But I'm not sure..."

Darting under the table isn't an option, but I can escape to the van outside. "Well, I'd better get going." I pick up the rooster painting. "Do you want this back?"

Carter's mom shakes her head. "Nope. Those paintings were bought and paid for. Your dad was a good man. Carter, walk Sophie to her car."

"OK. Come on, Boomer!" The dog leaps forward and leads us into the bright sunshine.

"So...I know this is weird," I say. "But I'm trying to understand my dad and the things he kept. He had seven of these hanging in his office." I hold up the rooster painting.

He smiles. "Seven. That's a lot of roosters."

"Yeah...." I can't get to the van fast enough. "Does she paint other animals?"

"Nope. Just roosters."

"Does she like farms? Why roosters?"

"She painted a lot of things before my dad left, but only roosters since then." He pauses. "I don't know why. What is it about roosters?"

As if I would know. I hardly even know the difference between roosters and chickens. I've sacrificed my self-respect to solve one mystery, and it's just led to another.

CHAPTER 37

Day 60. Yoga

I've tried, but I'm still not satisfied being un-notable. In other words, I'm full of ordinary and I don't know how to change it. I need advice.

I find GC in the family room, sitting on a kitchen chair following the movements of a young blonde on the TV. The woman's hands are tucked under her chin, and her elbows flutter up and down. "Do the butterfly," she calls to an imaginary audience.

GC has been acting strangely since Thanksgiving. Last night she cooked a "healthy" quinoa casserole and our cookie jar has been empty for approximately eighteen days. I'm really anxious for her to get over this phase.

"GC, tell me the truth. Are you a Russian spy?" I figure she's more likely to tell the truth if she's distracted.

She laughs and her elbows flutter up and down. "Where'd you get that idea, love?"

"Well, I'm still trying to figure out why the news guy called you."

"It's really nothin' sweetie."

She's *still* not ready to fess up. It's fine. I can be patient. I will win this battle eventually.

"How do people find things they're good at?" I change the subject.

"What do you like to do? Folks are usually good at things they like to do. I like to cook, and I'm quite good at it, if I say so myself."

She winks at me quickly and then obeys the instructor's command to *assume the cactus pose.*

"Well," I say. "I like to read. I guess I could be a professional reader. But only good books. I hate it when you have to read something boring for school that you hate and it just makes you sleepy and you can't even remember what you read five minutes ago."

GC looks like she's about to topple over. "Boring reading is bad. What else do you like to do?"

I think about that for a while. "Sometimes I like to write. On Thanksgiving I wrote an essay that I might enter into a contest."

"That's great!" GC has dropped to her hands and knees. She cranes her neck to look up at me. She doesn't look comfortable.

"But I haven't written anything else, not a book or anything."

"There is a first for everything," says GC, arching her back. "That's the thing about living. You can always stretch yourself and learn something new. Want to try some yoga?"

"You make it look very tempting, but no thanks."

I have a lot to think about. Authors are definitely important enough to be on Netopedia. And how hard can it be to write a book? You sit at a computer for a few hours, type out a story, and voila, you're famous. I search for a new pencil with an eraser that hasn't been bitten off, open my List notebook, and turn to the Becoming Netopedia Notable page.

#8 Be a Famous Author
    a. Think of a story.
    b. Write a book.

I think about writing my essay, how easily the words flowed onto the paper. I put the point of the pencil on the paper and wait for the book to come to me. I wait for a good two minutes. Nothing. Nothing new anyway. Just like everything else, all the good ideas have been taken. A book about kids at a wizard school? Check. Vampires? Done. Fairies and monsters and magical creatures and Greek gods? Someone has already thought of all of those. I can't think of anything new, nothing at all, and my pencil refuses to move on its own. I think that ideas must be like space on the earth or pieces of a pie. They are limited. And after thousands of years of ideas, and millions of books, they've all been used.

I'm back at square one. Less than square one. I'm at zero. Which is where nobodies stay. I rip the Netopedia Notable page out of the notebook and tear it into tiny pieces.

Practical Rules for Life

9. Sometimes you have to change your plans. And rip up lists.

CHAPTER 38

Day 61. A Special Surprise

On the morning of the dance, I spend extra time blow drying my hair, brushing on mascara, and putting on a new t-shirt. I stick a miniature bottle of mouthwash in my backpack next to my germ-killing gel, and head out. GC's already in the van honking for me.

Morning classes crawl by, but when we traipse into the gym after lunch, I have a feeling that it will be worth the wait. Tiny Christmas lights dangle from the basketball nets and white balloons blanket the floor like soft snow. White crepe paper streams from the middle of the floor to all four corners. It almost doesn't feel like a gym.

"The student council did a good job decorating," I murmur to Mia.

She nods, her eyes mirroring the twinkling lights.

A rap song blasts from the side of the gym. Two speakers are on each side of a table, where a teenage boy sits. I stare at him. He looks like one of Trevor's friends. He sees me staring and waves. I'm confused, because Trevor's friends have never acknowledged me before, but I wave back.

"Who is that?" whispers Mia.

"No one. Just one of Trevor's friends. I think his name might be Brian," I feel slightly important.

"He must be the DJ," she says. Brian does not look like the DJs in the movies. He should be surrounded by important looking electronic stuff, his hand on a record player. Instead, Brian is sitting behind an empty table. A long cord hangs from the phone in his hand. He swipes the screen and a new song starts.

The song is loud, with lots of thumping. The bass is turned up so high my liver jiggles and my head thumps. I think of the commercials about hearing aids and wonder if staying in this room for longer than thirty seconds will cause permanent damage to my ears.

We move to the wall where other groups of girls have gathered. I bounce to the beat of a new song and try not to glance in the direction of the boys. I don't want to look desperate.

According to Mia, who has spent a lot of time telling us the unwritten rules of dances, it's ok for groups to make a circle and dance during a fast song. Mia, Ashley, and I form a small circle a few feet away from the wall to dance. We are joined by a couple of other girls.

When a slow song starts playing, the dancing stops. Our circle moves to the side of the gym and stands there awkwardly until a few nervous guys come into enemy territory to ask girls to dance. The couples congregate in the center of the floor and sway. It hardly looks like dancing to me, but I hardly know anything about dancing. I spot Carter on the boys' side. He's talking and laughing with a group of his friends, and I force myself to look away.

After a few songs, I notice that our esteemed DJ has a pattern. Two loud fast songs and then a slow song. The fast songs are fine (except that I can't stop thinking that I am growing deaf by the minute) but the slow songs are really awkward, except for girls with boyfriends like Ashley (who looks like she's having a great time with Damian) and Emily Partridge's group.

Another song starts, and the same couples head to the middle of the floor to slow dance. Mr. Robinson, the PE teacher, steps in front of Carter's group of friends. Mr. Robinson's back is to me and I can't hear what he says (the hearing loss has already started. I am partially deaf). His hand gestures say he's not happy with something. He points in our direction.

I step closer to Mia and laugh as if she said something funny. I am still pretending to laugh when a Maddie Miller love song starts playing and Carter walks over to us.

"Hey Pop Rock," he says.

"Hey Rooster Rico," I answer.

"Want to dance?" he asks. I ignore Mia's laser stare and follow Carter to the middle of the gym. He puts his hands on my hips and starts shuffling his feet back and forth, turning in a slow circle. He's a little shorter than me, but I lace my fingers together behind his neck and try to match his shuffle.

I thought we were sort of friends, but that was before I stalked him and showed up at his house. Now we're at a school dance and I'm a stalker. That's a double serving of awkward. I search for something to say.

"How's Lilly?"

He brightens. "She scored a goal on Saturday."

"That's great!"

"Yeah, she was really excited."

We shuffle in awkward silence until the music ends.

"Thanks." He drops his hands from my hips.

"AND NOW, A SURPRISE…"

The voice thunders through the gym, clanging through the tiny strung lights, making it feel more like a basketball game than a dance.

"A SONG FROM A SPECIAL GUEST. ONE OF YOUR OWN…"

He pauses for dramatic effect.

My mind races.

A song from one of your own.

Trevor's friend Brian is the DJ.

The practice song I recorded.

Trevor and all of his friends heard it.

I back away from Carter, hoping against hope that…

"SOPHIE MURPHY!" Brian thunders.

He starts the song, and my screeching voice fills the air. Kids look at each other in stunned silence, and then someone starts laughing.

So does Carter. "What in the world?"

"Ummm…" I sputter.

I can't move. I'm paralyzed, and it has come at a very inopportune time.

You've abandoned me.

Alone I fight the demons you created.

I remember this part of the song. The girl in the song—me—is obviously sad. When I sang those words I was trying to put my soul into it. Now it is. My soul is in agony.

Carter touches my arm, and I remember how to move. I head for the exit, almost tripping in my haste.

He grabs my arm to stop me. "Wait."

I stand in the middle of the gym floor, laughter and confusion surrounding me. I watch Carter walk to the table where Brian is laughing so hard he can't stand straight. Carter picks up Brian's phone and yanks the cord from the bottom.

"Come on," he says to me, and I follow him out of the gym.

CHAPTER 39

Day 61 (continued). Disappointment

My heart pounds and my hands shake, but my brain is frozen. It's stuck in the gym and can't even comprehend what just happened. I clench my fists to stop the shaking from spreading, but I'm too late and my entire body starts to shake. Even my teeth clatter. It's like I'm standing outside in the middle of a Minnesota winter.

"Are you ok?" asks Carter, who is walking next to me.

I'd forgotten about him.

I clench my jaw, forget how to walk, and trip on a joint in the sidewalk.

"Sophie," He grabs my arm, steadying me. "Are you ok?"

"That stupid Brian." I'm no longer cold. I'm shaking with rage. "How'd he get to be the DJ anyway?

I turn with fury on Carter. "How did that happen?"

He shrugs, a slight smile on his face, like he wants to laugh but doesn't dare. "I'm really confused," he admits.

My mind races. "I'm not sure where to start."

"Singing?" he suggests.

"Yes, singing. But it started before that." I'm not sure I want to tell him the entire story: the failures, the falls. The details are too embarrassing. I take a deep, shaky breath.

"It all started with Netopedia. My dad wasn't on there."

"Really?" Carter says. "I thought everyone was on there."

"No. I emailed to tell them to include my Dad, but they said they only have *notable*, *important* people. And my Dad wasn't one of those. And neither was I."

I wipe tears from my eyes before they can fall. "Neither *am* I. So I thought maybe if I did something important..."

"Wait," he says. "Football?"

I nod. "But it started with gymnastics."

He laughs. "Gymnastics. You were there with the little kids. You landed on Lilly."

"Yes," I admit. "And I thought maybe I could be a singer, so I recorded myself singing. My brother and his friends got the recording..."

"And they played it for the entire school," he finishes.

"Yes. Thank you for laying it out there."

He laughs. "Sorry."

"Can you believe they did that? And my very own brother? Just stabbed me in the back. Threw me under the bus." I try to think of another way to say it. The words don't come close to describing my anger.

"Unacceptable," Carter agrees.

"Yes."

We walk in silence while my brain works its way through it.

"I didn't know that you're a singer," Carter offers, after a while.

I laugh. "I'm not. Obviously."

I take a shaky breath. "What am I doing to do? What now?"

He squints in the bright sunlight. "I don't know. You could hide in embarrassment. Or you could pick yourself up and move on. Everyone has disappointments and embarrassing moments. Two years ago I was playing in a game and I caught an interception."

He glances at me, maybe remembering my knowledge of football. "That means I caught a pass that was meant for the other side. After I caught it, I heard the cheers from my team and the parents on the sidelines, and I was pumped. But I was so pumped, I sort of lost my mind and ran to the wrong end zone. *I scored a touchdown for the other team.* The coaches yelled at me, parents laughed, my team teased me for days. And I wanted to quit football."

He stops for a minute. I wait. I learned that from Dr. Williams.

"I don't even like football that much. I play because my friends play. I'd rather play soccer."

I nod. "Me too. But you went back to football."

"Yeah. I decided that I wasn't going to let one measly mistake win. I wasn't going to let it decide whether or not I quit. If I quit, it would be because I didn't want to play football anymore. But not because I was too embarrassed to step back on the field."

I consider that for the next block. "Is that your biggest disappointment?"

"No. My biggest disappointment is that my Dad left."

I nod. "Me too."

We walk silently to 2232 Mesa Verde Drive.

I stop, unsure. I want the day to end but not this conversation. "This is my house."

"Ok." He looks me in the eye. "Are you ok?"

"Yeah. Except I've got to figure out how to get Trevor back."

"You should do something with this." He presses Brian's phone into my hand.

I drop it in my pocket. "Thanks for rescuing me."

He shrugs. "Everyone needs to be rescued once in a while."

I watch him walk away. I could offer him a cookie, but we don't have those anymore. And offering a friend a protein ball just isn't the same.

CHAPTER 40

Day 61 (continued again). Flaxseed Muffins ≠ Blueberry Muffins

I explain to Mom and GC why I'm home early, but I leave out the part about Carter walking me home. Not because it wasn't great, but because it's a happy thing I want to keep to myself for a little while.

GC brings me a flaxseed muffin.

"... and that's why I may quit school to become a professional *Price is Right* contestant."

"Sophie Murphy," Mom says, and I know what's coming.

"Of course she's going back," GC interrupts. "Sophie is the toughest girl I know. She's not going to let that...Brian win, the slimy eel..."

She pauses and I know what's coming, because it always does. In GC's world, it's ok to speak your mind about anyone, as long as you bless that person's heart. I wait for it.

"...Bless his heart. When I see that boy again, I'll mix him up like jambalaya. Sophie's going to pretend like nothing ever happened, like he didn't get under her skin one bit."

I'm too tired to argue. I feel like I've taken a roller coaster ride and I just want to stand on solid ground for a little while.

GC, Mom, and I settle into the sofa with pillows and blankets for a Harry Potter movie marathon, and for the next six hours, we only move to order pizza and open more cans of soda. Ollie joins us between headstands and his Matchbox car races. Trevor doesn't come home.

All night I think about what Carter said. He refused to quit football, not because he liked it, but because he refused to give up. I'm horrified to go back to school, to face all those people who heard my song. But I shouldn't let dumb Brian have that much power. I should take control of my life back. If I become a professional *Price is Right* contestant, it should be because that's what I want, not by default.

I can be tough. Like Carter was. Like GC thinks I am. I don't want to go back, and I don't feel tough, but maybe I should 'fake it 'til I make it', as GC says.

And then I think of roosters, and I spend the next hour watching videos of them on the computer.

CHAPTER 41

Day 62. We Are Still A Family

Mia calls me Saturday afternoon. "Carter asked you to dance!" she wails. "Tell me everything. How was it? Did you talk to him?"

"I'm sorry, Mia. I know you wanted to dance with him. I don't blame you—he's a nice guy."

"It's ok," she says. "I sort of like Liam too, and he asked me to dance, and then he told me 'Thanks.' I think he might like me."

"That's good. Liam's cute."

I wait...

...for a few seconds, but then I have to get it out. "And the song?"

"What song?"

My insides untwist. Maybe if Mia doesn't remember, others don't either. And the most embarrassing moment of my life can disappear into oblivion.

"My song," I remind her. "The song Brian played?"

"Oh. Yeah." She giggles. I shouldn't have reminded her.

"That was really funny. You totally mocked Maddie Miller. It was awful. And hilarious."

"You disappeared," she says. "I didn't see you after your song. Where did you go?"

"I got tired and came home. And I was pretty embarrassed," I allow.

"Why? It was obviously a joke."

I want to hug Mia.

"You didn't miss anything. The dance ended because the dumb DJ lost his phone with his music on it. The teachers were so mad at him they called the high school and the principal gave him lunch detention for the rest of December."

Trevor emerges from his room on Sunday, and Mom joins him at the kitchen table. I'm walking through the hall when I hear them.

"Even if Dad is gone, we are still a family. We are a family that sticks together. We stick up for each other. I'd be disappointed if you played a mean prank like that on anyone, but that you did it to your sister makes it even worse. You will apologize to your sister, and you will attend therapy for your anger issues."

"Mom!" I hear Trevor protest. "I told you before, I'm not going to talk to some guy about my problems."

"You will go," says Mom. "And maybe you should talk about how you treat members of your family. Because your behavior lately has been entirely unacceptable."

I agree. His behavior has been entirely unacceptable.

And probably unforgiveable.

CHAPTER 42

Day 64. Proud

I'm not sure why I was so worried about going back to school on Monday. Only a few people tease me. Mostly the dumb football players, and I don't care what they think anyway.

I see Carter in the hall after math. "I've been doing some research on roosters," I tell him.

"About roosters?"

"Yeah, what's so special about roosters. And why your mom would want to paint them."

"Oh," he says. "I haven't thought about roosters at all. I try not to, in fact."

"Well, I have. And here's what I've decided. Most of the barnyard animals walk. The rooster struts. And have you ever heard a rooster?"

Carter stares at me like I've lost a screw. "No. Not in real life."

"Me either. But I watched a video. A rooster wakes up in the morning singing, and it's not a pretty sound. But he doesn't care, he does it anyway. Your mom's paintings all show roosters who hold their heads up high because they're proud to be roosters."

"Yes," says Carter slowly. "That explains a lot."

He grins at me. "Does that mean you're going to be a singer?"

"Nope. I've moved on. Although I'm not sure where yet. I'm hoping I've already hit the low point."

CHAPTER 43

Day 66. ~~Revenge~~ Lessons

"Sophie," yells Trevor from the family room where a basketball game blares from the TV. "Brian wants his phone back."

I forgot I had that stupid phone. I haven't seen or thought about it since the dance.

"Why would I have Brian's phone?" I answer innocently.

GC snaps to attention. "Yes indeed. Why would Sophie have Brian's phone?"

"He saw you walk out of the gym with it and he wants it back," says Trevor. "It has all of his music and photos and stuff."

I walk into my bedroom, rummage through my sock drawer and pull the phone from its sock home. I don't hold a grudge, but I owe it to any future girls in Brian's life to teach him a lesson.

You just don't treat people like that, and you never underestimate the power of a twelve-year-old girl.

I'm surprised the phone still has power, and that it doesn't have a password. Apparently, Brian didn't consider the possibility that someone would confiscate his phone. I find his recordings, delete all of them just to make sure my song is gone forever, and empty the trash file.

Then I stare at the phone.

Inspiration does not arrive, so naturally, I start a new list.

~~How to Get Revenge~~ *How to teach an object lesson*
1. *Things Trevor and his stinky friends like*
   —*cars*
   —*phones*
   —*food*

I consider cars: If I were a character in a book or a movie, I'd cut their brakes. Except I'm not a character, and I'm not evil enough to wish them dead. And who knows how to do that kind of stuff anyway?

I could do something with eggs or toilet paper or shaving cream, but I feel like they'd see it, laugh, and run to the car wash. No one learns lessons from shaving cream.

Phones. That's a possibility. I have Brian's phone, after all. I earned it fair and square with my suffering. I should make use of it.

Food. It occurs to me that Trevor and his friends like food more than anything. The brains of sixteen-year-old boys are mush where food is concerned.

I bite the eraser off the end of the pencil.

What if I combined Brian's phone with food?

In a flash, inspiration comes. I find GC and pull her into my bedroom to whisper my plan. GC doesn't believe in revenge either, but she understands lessons that will benefit aspiring singers and little sisters everywhere.

She walks back into the kitchen. "Trevor," she calls. "I'd like to invite you to a special dinner."

Trevor's eyes bulge as they usually do when food is mentioned, especially when it's GC's cooking. "Awesome, Grandma! When?"

"This Friday. Invite all of your friends, especially those who might be hungry from skipping lunch."

I don't think Trevor picks up on the clue that GC's referring to a certain friend who has lunch detention. Or maybe he underestimates GC.

That's a big mistake if you ask me.

CHAPTER 44

Day 68. Turkey, the Second Time

I rush home from school on Friday to help GC with dinner, but when I get there the turkey is already in the oven and the rolls and pies are cooling on the counter. Once again she asks me to peel potatoes. This time I don't complain.

I watched a nature movie about bears once. When the winter snow started to melt, the bear came out of his den. He glanced around, sniffed the air, and headed to find food. He was oblivious to everything but dinner.

I think of that bear when I see Trevor's friends crowd the kitchen at 6:00. They're ready to scarf down anything in sight.

"It's almost ready," says GC as sweet as a chocolate cream pie. "Have a seat at the table."

GC and I load the table with plates of mashed potatoes, gravy, rolls, and salad, and then GC makes a grand entrance with the turkey. The turkey looks like it came from the pages of a magazine. It is golden brown, glistening, arranged in the middle of a plate surrounded by sprigs of green plants and red berries. I know what's inside but the smell still makes my stomach rumble.

"Happy Turkey Day!" GC says. She puts the turkey in the middle of the table and gazes at it fondly, as if it's a masterpiece.

"Ummm Grandma?" says Trevor. "Thanksgiving passed a few weeks ago. Remember? Today is December 20?" He looks at GC like she's lost her marbles.

"I know love," she says. "But we eat turkeys on other days too."

She eyes Brian. "We eat them. Gobble them up."

Brian smiles faintly. He looks confused and I actually feel a little sorry for him. He thinks he teased a twelve-year-old mouse. He doesn't realize that he's up against a massive mama bear.

GC hands Trevor the carving knife and he stands, ready to slice.

"Ummm, what is that inside the turkey?" Matt, who is sitting next to Brian, points.

Trevor jabs at the skin on the neck, and eight boys around the table crane their necks to see. Trevor reaches in and pulls out the plastic and metal object, which glistens with turkey fat.

"Owww!" He flings it to the floor. "It's hot!" He shakes his hand and blows on his forefinger and thumb.

"It would be," says GC calmly. "It was baked for six hours."

All of the eyes in the room turn to the object lying on the floor.

"Is that...my phone?" whimpers Brian.

I smile. Revenge is sweet.

It only takes minutes for the shock of the phone to wear off (well, for everyone but Brian) and then their instincts kick in. They become bears consuming their first spring meal, not even caring that deadly toxins were probably released into the turkey from a phone baking inside of it.

CHAPTER 45

Day 71. Baked Phones

"I took care of the phone," I tell Carter before Social Studies on Monday. His eyes widen. "How?"

Mrs. Bowen starts class before I can tell him.

He's waiting for me outside after school. "Sophie."

I stop and motion for Mia to go on without me.

"What'd you do?"

I tell him about the baked turkey.

He whistles. "Did you really bake his phone?"

"I probably should have, but I lost my nerve. I'm sort of a wimp," I admit. "But phones are expensive. So we baked Ollie's toy phone. It looks a lot like Brian's, and I thought he'd never be able to tell the difference, especially if it was covered in turkey goop. I was right. Brian thought it was his phone, and I haven't given him his real phone back yet."

Carter laughs. "You're a beast, Sophie. You're a *rooster*."

I've accomplished one mission. With one swoop I basically called Brian a turkey and scared the living daylights out of him. GC would say that's "killing two birds with one stone."

CHAPTER 46

Day 73. Coping Mechanisms

Since Trevor has started therapy, Mom stacks our appointments and makes him drive me. It works out well for her, not so great for Trevor and me.

"Fine," I told Mom when she informed me of the new arrangements. "But Trevor has to drive the van. I am not riding with Trevor in Dad's car."

"Fine," Trevor said. "I'm not using my gas for stupid therapy anyway."

I wait in the lobby while Trevor therapies. He glares at me when he comes out, like it's my fault he's here. "Your turn," he growls. He's still angry about the turkey. I feel some satisfaction. I find some joy in making Trevor slightly miserable.

Dr. Williams shuts the door behind me and sits on his desk.

"How have you been?"

"I'm fine," I tell him. "Except I don't think I need therapy anymore. Congratulations, Dr. Williams, you cured me."

"Oh, I think we still have some issues to cover."

I study him. "Like what?" Maybe he knows more than I do.

"Well, your mother mentioned recently that you consistently read the obituaries."

Of course she did. Mom's usually late to the game. "I don't do that anymore."

"Why did you start reading them in the first place?"

"I just wanted to see what people accomplished. I wanted to see if they were complete and ready to die."

"Interesting. Why are you not compelled to do that anymore?"

I shrug. "I just don't think about it. I'm too busy."

He waits, staring at me, and I shift uncomfortably. "Maybe the middle became more important than the end. I was missing the middle because I spent so much time thinking about the end."

He considers that.

"Do you have any other coping mechanisms?"

He calls himself a child psychologist and he says things like *coping mechanisms*? Anyone who knows anything about kids knows that you don't say words like that.

"Habits," he clarifies. "Do you have other habits?"

"I make lists. Practical Rules for Life. Things I Need To Do. Just step by step lists of how to accomplish things."

"How does that help you?"

"I'm not sure."

Naturally, he waits.

"I guess it makes huge things seem smaller. Manageable."

"Interesting."

"And the Practical Rules are things I need to remember. Things I've learned. I write them down so I don't make the same mistakes again. They're very useful, and... practical."

"Hmmm." He glances at his watch. "Well, we've run out of time. We'll explore that in your next visit."

Trevor and I ride home in silence.

CHAPTER 47

Day 75. The Important Side

I wake up early in the morning, and I don't even have to think of an excuse to stay in bed. It is Friday, the last day of school before Christmas vacation, and everyone can get through one day. It's an easy day anyway—no assignments, no tests— basically there's no learning.

In math class, the loudspeaker interrupts Ms. Dudley's lecture on integers. (Really? Integers on the last day of class before Christmas break?) "Ms. Dudley, please send Sophie Murphy to the office," the crackling voice orders.

I smush paper into my notebook and stand up. I don't know why I've been summoned, but it makes no difference. Good or bad, it gets me out of math. I take my time walking down the hallway, just to maximize the minutes of freedom. A sprung prisoner doesn't hurry back to her cell.

"Ah Sophie," says the attendance secretary when I push open the office door. "Mr. Gomez would like to see you. Go right in." I look toward the office and take back my ambivalence. Any visit to the principal's office is bad news.

"Hello, Sophie," says Mr. Gomez. He nods toward the chairs that face his desk. "Have a seat."

I sit.

"How are you doing?"

"I am fine." Since I arrived in his office, my throat has started hurting. I may have laryngitis, but I'll spare him the news.

"Good." He wipes the top of his shiny bald head. "I called you in to congratulate you. Your essay was chosen as the first place winner of the Impressions contest. It will now proceed to the regional level."

"That's great, Mr. Gomez. Thanks for letting me know." I stand up, hoping that we are finished. This place makes me nervous.

I walk through the open door and then turn back as something occurs to me. "Mr. Gomez? What is the prize for winning?" I'm expecting a blue ribbon stapled to a paper certificate or a coupon for a free scoop of ice cream.

I'm right. He hands me a copy of my essay with an attached ribbon. My shoulders sag.

"But that isn't all!" He gets up from his desk and walks toward me. "Come with me. I'll show you."

He leads me out of the office, walks toward the main entry, and stops when he reaches the trophy case that faces the front doors. I guess someone must look inside this thing, but it has never been me. Although it's easy to ignore, it's not because of its size. It is taller than Mr. Gomez and as wide as the three sets of double doors at the entrance of the school. Three wood shelves sit behind glass. The shelves are lined with gleaming trophies and wooden plaques. I see photos of smiling cheerleaders shaking red and yellow pompoms, a dingy white net next to a photo of a basketball team from 2002, and a trophy with a gleaming gold football perched at the top.

"I know I shouldn't play favorites," said Mr. Gomez in a solemn museum voice. "But this section is my favorite. These are the academic awards."

He points to the section at the end of the case. *The nerd section*, I think. The awards here are different. Regional Math League Champions 2008-2009. State Blue Ribbon School.

He takes a large ring of keys from his pocket and thumbs through them until he finds a small silver key. He sticks the key into the lock, slides open a glass window, and takes a large wood plaque from the second shelf. Stretched across the top of the plaque is a metal plate engraved with the words Treasure Valley Middle School Impressions Winners. Gold metal rectangles are lined in two rows. Jessica Garcia-2000 is engraved on the first square.

I point to the empty square below 2019. "Will my name be there?"

Mr. Gomez nods. "It will. And this plaque will sit on the important side of the case for every student and visitor to see."

Did he just say **important side***?* I think as I walk back to math class. My name will be written on the *important* side of the trophy case for all the world to see. That might be just as good as ending up in the National Obituaries. I wonder if regional Impressions contest winners have their own Netopedia pages. But maybe I'm counting my chickens before they've hatched, as GC would say.

CHAPTER 48

Day 75 (continued). Vacuums

I'm sitting in Language Arts when the loudspeaker buzzes again. "Mrs. Pringle, is Sophie Murphy in your class? Will you have her come to the office?"

Mr. Gomez probably forgot to give me the ice cream coupon, I think as I gather up my things.

"Your mother called," says the secretary when I walk through the door. "She said that your grandmother has had a medical emergency and they are at the hospital. You are to walk home after school."

"What does that mean—medical emergency?" I ask, my heart thumping wildly.

"I don't have any more information, sweetie," she says. "But there is nothing you can do now, except to be patient."

I shuffle out of the office, thinking of every disease, every illness I've ever read about. GC could have any of those. GC could end up like my dad. I could lose them both. *I could lose them both.* My brain races and my face burns. I walk into the bathroom, turn the cold water on, and stick my head in the running water. *Nothing you can do, Sophie.* I tell myself as the water runs over my face.

Even if I can't do anything to help her now, I can't stay here and pretend everything is normal. I grab my backpack, and for the second time in a month, I walk out of the school in tears.

When I get home I search each room but I can't find any clues. No blood, no broken glass, no outline of a body drawn onto the floor, no sign that a catastrophe or a 'medical emergency' took place here. The only thing that's out of place in the entire house is the vacuum laying on the floor in the middle of the living room. "What do you know, vacuum?"

It refuses to give up its secrets. I've always hated that thing.

I pace through the house. 50 steps down the hall into Mom's room, 50 steps back.

I think about my dad and how much I miss him, and then I think about GC. She can't leave me too. I kick the silent vacuum and walk into GC's room to smell her.

I'm laying on GC's bed when I hear honking. I run out to see Dad's Honda on the street in front of our house. I motion for Trevor to roll down the passenger window.

I lean into the car. "GC is sick!"

He nods. "I know. I was at the hospital, and Mom asked me to pick up Ollie from preschool." He motions to the back seat, where I see Ollie, small in the seat belt.

"Can you take him? I've got to get back. Mom looks like crap."

I'm surprised he noticed. Mom has looked like crap since May 5th.

I open the door and unbuckle Ollie.

"Sophie?" Trevor says before I can shut the door.

"Yeah?"

"I'm sorry about the dance."

I hold Ollie's hand as I watch Trevor pull away. There's a new sticker on the back window of the Honda. It's a guitar. I smile, understanding. Trevor is still driving Dad's car, and I still haven't forgiven him for that (it's obviously a coping mechanism), but at least he's acknowledged Dad.

CHAPTER 49

Day 75 (it goes on and on).
Hearts

"How was your day, knucklehead?" I ruffle Ollie's hair.

"Good. Where is Grammie?"

"She's sick."

He nods. "Like Daddy?"

"Nope," I say, more bravely than I feel. "Not like Dad at all."

"Ohhh. Sick like Luis who barfed on the rug."

"Yep," I say. "Just like Luis. She'll probably be better tomorrow."

Ollie and I walk into the house and turn on the TV. When it gets dark, I make scrambled eggs for Ollie and give him a bath and scratch his back until he falls asleep. Then I lie in the dark until, at last, I hear the garage door open. I meet Mom in the kitchen. She's alone.

"Where is she?" I ask. I had hoped to see GC walk in behind her with a bandaged thumb, grumbling about her clumsiness with a knife.

Mom sighs and rubs her forehead like she's trying to erase her memory of the day. "In the hospital. She had a heart attack."

"What?" I have not done any research on heart attacks, but I have heard of them. Mr. Garcia, who lived three houses down the street, died from a heart attack a year ago.

"What exactly is a heart attack? Medically speaking?" I need more information and I want it directly from a reliable source. Preferably not the internet, because it exaggerates.

Mom looks tired but she humors me. "Blood vessels carry oxygen to your heart. Sometimes those vessels are blocked and oxygen can't get to your heart. Cells in your heart die when they don't get enough oxygen."

"How much of Grandma's heart died?"

"I don't know, Sophie. Luckily, I was home when it happened and we were able to get to the hospital quickly. Tomorrow she'll have an angiography and probably an angioplasty."

"What?" I yell. "GC's having a nose job? Now is not the time for a nose job!"

Mom stares at me, and then she throws her head back and starts to laugh—a deep, belly laugh. She's acting crazier than a road lizard, but who can blame her. She has been dealing with a lot of stress.

"You make me laugh," Mom says.

I'm irritated because I didn't say anything funny. I mean, sometimes I am pretty funny. But I'm funny when I mean to be. And this time I definitely did not mean to be. This is serious stuff and does not call for laughing.

"Grandma is not having a nose job," she says at last. "An angioplasty is when doctors stick a balloon into the blood vessel and inflate it to clear out the blockage."

"Oh," I feel dumb, but now is not the time to think about my feelings. I follow Mom as she walks up the stairs to Ollie's room. "How is she feeling? When can I see her?"

"She's tired. We'll know more tomorrow."

CHAPTER 50

Day 76. Anxious

Mom is gone when I wake up. She's gone while Ollie and I watch Saturday morning veterinary shows on TV. She's gone when we cover the kitchen table with homemade corn starch slime. She's not home to object to our ramen noodle lunch. She's not home when I start researching heart attack symptoms and treatments.

I read about the symptoms of a heart attack and my chest tightens. "It's in your head, Sophie," I whisper over and over again. Treatment plans look complicated, so I make notecards with options and study them while Ollie watches multiple episodes of Trainland.

When Mom walks through the door at dinner time, I've had enough. "Well?" I stand in front of her with my hands on my hips. "What do you have to report? And why haven't you called?"

"Sorry," Mom says as she kneels on the floor with her arms around a slightly dirty Ollie. "It was a crazy day. The tests showed that her heart is not very healthy…"

"Is she taking angiotensin receptor neurolysin inhibitors?" I blurt before it leaves my brain for good.

"What?" Mom glances at me sideways.

"What did you say?" Her words are finally registering in my brain. "The tests were not good?"

"No. She's in heart failure. Turns out that a steady diet of croissants, bacon, and Dr. Pepper is not good for your heart. She's scheduled for bypass surgery the first week of January."

"When can I see her?"

"Tomorrow. She's anxious to see you."

CHAPTER 51

Day 77. GC

I watch Phineas and Ferb until midnight, and then I try to sleep. I wake up at 2:42 and 4:27. At 7:03, I pull on jeans and a sweater, put my LISTS notebook and essay inside my backpack and walk into Mom's room. She's sleeping on the right side of the bed, inches away from the edge even though it's king-sized. Ollie's snuggled next to her.

"Mom!" I lean down to whisper. "Are you awake?" It's not until I ask that I realize it's not a very good question.

She moans.

"What time can I go see GC?" I'm trying to whisper. Still, Ollie stirs.

"After ten. Come get in bed." I stare at the empty spot on the left side. Dad's spot, where the covers and pillow lay stiff and untouched.

"I can't sleep there." No one should ever sleep there. Ever again.

She pushes Ollie over a few inches and scoots next to him, leaving empty the small space where she just slept. It is, however, the warm sleepable side. "Come on, Sophie, get in."

I pull off my backpack, snuggle next to her and doze until 10:05, when we leave Ollie with Trevor and drive to the hospital. Mom walks me to GC's room and stops, her hand on the doorknob. "Are you sure you can handle this?"

I know she's thinking about Dad. He was in the hospital five different times before he died, so we spent a lot of time here. Each time he came, a little more life was sucked out of him. When he died, I vowed to be finished with this place.

But it's not Dad in there. This time it's GC, and she's going to have a different ending. I meet Mom's eyes, swallow, and nod. Mom pushes the door open and I step inside room 315.

GC looks small and lonely in the hospital bed. Her skin is pale, almost translucent, the same color as the greyish-white sheets. Tubes stretch from her arms and chest to beeping machines on both sides of the bed. But it isn't the tubes, the beeps, or the mask covering the lower half of her face that freaks me out. It's her lips. They are not pink peony, but tinged bluish. GC's in bad shape.

I stand just inside the door, afraid to move forward. I want to run from this place. But GC turns her head toward me and through the mask I see her smile. My knees shake but I step forward. "Hi Grandma," I say softly.

"When did you start calling me Grandma?" Her voice rasps. She gasps for air and then she starts to cough. Her body shakes as she coughs. It is way too long before she relaxes. She takes a few deep breaths and then she looks at me again, as if she wants to say something.

"Don't talk," Mom orders. "Sophie's here to keep you company. I'm going home to shower. I'll be back in a couple of hours."

Since talking has been forbidden, GC and I both nod. I cling to her hand and listen to the machines beep. Her chest rises as she sucks air into her lungs. After a few minutes, I can't listen anymore. I start to talk, to say anything to cover up the sound of the machines.

"We're waiting for you to get home to have our Christmas. Mom, Trevor, and I don't really want to celebrate without you. Ollie has no idea what day it is. He wants a robot dinosaur. I...the only thing I want is for you to be well." My voice cracks. I'm too close to the edge of an abyss. I tell myself to back up, to talk about something normal.

"School is out until January 7. On the last day of school, the principal called me to the office to tell me that I won the Impressions contest. I wrote an essay. Do you want to hear it?"

I pull my backpack from under my chair and take the paper out. I push back the blue ribbon to read the words on the page.

A towering oak lives in my Grandma's front yard. It is the first thing I glimpse when I arrive at her house and the last thing I see when I have to tell her goodbye when we leave Minnesota. The tree has been there for as long as I can remember. Its upper branches reach far into the sky, further than any chimney around. Each branch spreads in its own direction, each reaches for a different goal. The branches are different but they all have the same oak leaves.

In the summer you imagine that the tree can't live without its leaves. They shield the delicate branches from the blinding sun, absorb light and send energy to the trunk. The leaves allow the tree to live.

But when the summer sun disappears and the bitter winds blow in, the tree loses its leaves. They *are carried off by the wind, leaving the branches lonely and bare.*

Without its leaves the tree shrivels. It sleeps, hiding from the ugliness of the world. Eventually when the sunlight warms the ground again the tree may recover. It may live and grow again. But first it needs some time to mourn the loss of its leaves.

My Dad was leaves for Mom, Trevor, Ollie and me. He...

The words on the page go on, but I stop. The tears on my cheeks and the lump in my throat make it impossible to read them. GC sucks in oxygen but she doesn't need to speak. Her eyes say it all. She understands. I grip her fingers tighter and I lay my head next to our hands and I close my eyes.

CHAPTER 52

Day 77 (continued). Splatters of Tomato Sauce

I am still holding GC's hand when Mom shakes me awake. I lift my head not knowing where I am, but then I hear the beeping and remember. And at the same time, I want to forget.

"I guess I fell asleep," I whisper to Mom. She smiles down at me and nods.

"You look better," I tell her. She does. She's not rumpled and wrinkly anymore, and although there are still bags under her eyes, at least she looks clean.

Together we watch GC's chest rise and fall. "She's not going to leave us, is she Mom?" I whisper. My mom has never lied to me. I know if I ask her a question, whether about if Santa is real or if my hair looks horrible or if Dad is going to die, she will tell me the truth.

"She will eventually," she says. "But I hope it's not time yet. I hope we have some time left." She squeezes my shoulders but then stops to reach for something on the floor.

"What's this?"

It's my essay. I yank it from her fingers and stuff it in my backpack. Me reading it to GC is one thing; Mom reading it is another. I'm embarrassed for her to see what I wrote. What I wrote felt too close, like I was cutting myself wide open and letting people come inside. Maybe it would be better to write a story that said nothing and meant nothing.

But this is too close and Mom's too far away.

"It's nothing," I say. "Just an essay I wrote for school. It must have fallen out of my backpack."

"Oh."

I see that I've hurt her feelings. I try to make it up to her and change the subject at the same time. "It's going to be ok, Mom. Grandma will come home and we'll have Christmas just like we always have."

She watches the beeping machines. "That's the problem, Sophie. Nothing will ever be the same again."

"I know." I lay my hand on top of hers. "I miss Dad too."

After a while, Mom drives me home. I walk in alone to find Trevor and Ollie sitting at the kitchen table. They're eating lasagna GC made and froze for later. They've left the microwave open, and I can see the splatters of tomato sauce inside. Dishes with crusty food are piled in the sink. I should clean up to help Mom, but I can't do it tonight. I'm not sleepy but I am so tired. I feel heavy, like if another thought comes into my head it might explode. I'm sure it's a symptom of a disease but I'll have to look it up tomorrow.

CHAPTER 53

Day 78. Netopedia

GC's bed is propped up when I walk into her hospital room. She frowns at the tray in front of her. "Did you bring me a croissant for breakfast?"

I kiss her cheek and look at the bowl of oatmeal on her tray. It looks disgusting, and I don't blame her for not eating it.

"You know you can't eat croissants," says Mom, though she's busy checking tubes and cords and machines.

"Well, I can't eat this...glue..." GC pushes the tray away, winks at me, and nestles back into her pillows. "I'm glad you're here," she says to me.

I turn on the TV and we watch *The Price is Right* while Mom buzzes around the room, doing important stuff. "Will you two be alright for a few minutes? I've got a couple of things to do," Mom interrupts the second showcase. GC and I are both too busy to care.

When I hear the music for *The Young and the Old*, I grab the remote from GC's tray and turn the volume down.

"You look much better today," I tell her. It's only a half-lie. Her skin is so pale I can see the veins running beneath it. She's been trying to hide her shaking hands, but she's lousy at keeping secrets. But pink peony is back on her lips where it belongs. That is definitely a good sign.

"I'm ready to break out of here," she says.

I know that is a complete lie because the small effort of watching TV and talking has left her exhausted.

She breathes deeply, and I see her chest rise and then fall. I think of how I would feel if it stayed still. The thought stops my own breath. If half of my heart died with Dad, the other half would go with GC.

She turns her head and studies me. "I loved your essay," she says like she can read my mind.

"Thanks." I duck my head. Even with her, I feel shy about it, and I can't look her in the eye.

"I know it's been hard for you with your Dad gone."

"It stinks. Please don't die, GC. I need you."

"I don't plan to leave you yet," she says. "But if I did, you'd be alright."

My throat tightens and I can't speak. I shake my head. *No, I would not be alright.*

"Do you ever wonder," I say after a while, "that you haven't made a big enough impact in the world? That the world would continue on without you just the same as it was before?"

She pauses. "No, I can't say I've thought about that."

I wait for her to think about it.

"I believe that I've made a big enough impact in my little world. I don't really care if the rest of the world knows I am gone. My life is important because I am important to you. You are enough," she says at last.

I think about that.

"You're right, you are important to me," I say a little while later. "But if you died, the world won't even know that you are gone. You would not be in the national obituaries."

She doesn't answer right away, and I'm worried that I've hurt her feelings. She lays her head back into her pillow and closes her eyes. I think maybe she didn't hear me. She breathes deeply, in and out, and then she says. "You think your Dad wasn't important because his obituary wasn't on the national page?"

How did she guess that? Even when she's sick, she's too sharp for her own good. I duck my head, embarrassed to admit it. It does sound kind of dumb when she says it out loud like that. "No," I tell her. "I just made a goal to be in Netopedia."

"Netopedia?" She lifts her head from the pillow to stare at me. She's frowning like she's confused. "You want to have a listing on Netopedia?"

How does she have this talent of making things sound ridiculous? Suddenly I see a resemblance between GC and my Mom.

"Well...yes..." I admit.

"Is that what the last few weeks have been about, Sophie? Netopedia?"

I don't answer.

"Fame is not all it's cracked up to be, sweet pea," she says. "The world out there, it'll suck you dry and then abandon you. People may read about you in the newspaper, but they don't really know you. And they definitely don't care about you."

I'm out of patience. She may be sick and weak, but she's won the battle of wills. "What do you know about fame, GC? You've been avoiding my questions about the news guy, you've been saying that it's nothing. You know what I think? I think you've never been famous. You're just a Grandma from Minnesota."

She waves me away. "I'm tired now, darlin'. You let me rest a spell. We'll talk more later."

She nestles her head into the pillow again and closes her eyes. I watch her chest rise and fall and listen to the beeps that fill the room until Mom comes to drive me home.

Her phone rings as we're pulling into the garage. She rummages through her bag to find it. "Hello, Edna. She's doing better, just weak. She did? Well, I guess she needs it then. You know where the key is?"

I wander into the house to meet Ollie.

I think about GC as I run Ollie's bubble bath. Maybe she shook the President's hand. Maybe she wrote an essay sixty years ago and her name was engraved on a plaque. Most likely her apple pie won a baking contest.

CHAPTER 54

Day 79. A Russian Spy

The FedEx guy brings a package to our house the next day. It's a square box addressed to GC from Minnesota. I put it on her empty bed and forget about it until I see her that night at the hospital.

"Open it," she says. "It's from my Russian spy network."

"Spies don't use FedEx," I tell her. I know because I've seen some spy movies. "They hide messages at the bottom of flower pots. Or something like that."

As soon as I get home, I open the package to find a burgundy colored three-ring binder. *Memories* is stenciled in gold lettering on the front. I turn the pages carefully. A baby photo. An ancient report card. A spelling list carefully printed in faded pencil.

And then a newspaper clipping with a photo of a young lady sitting on the hood of a car. Pinky Morgan is printed below the photo.

I run to the den, turn on the computer, and type Pinky Morgan in the search bar.

A Netopedia listing pops up. I click on it.

Pinky Morgan (January 7, 1945 - present) is an American stock car driver who gained fame as the first woman to win the Carolina 500. She was known professionally as "Pinky" for her diminutive size, the color of her signature helmet, her ever-present pink lipstick, and her appetite for speed. After her victory in the Carolina 500, Morgan became the pretty face of the American Stock Racing Circuit until she unexpectedly stepped away from the spotlight in 1968. She never reappeared, apparently relishing obscurity.

It is impossible. I read the listing again and then I stare at the photo on the right side of the screen. A young face peers back at me. The photo is black and white, and blurry, but I recognize those smiling eyes. They last smiled at me a few hours ago from a hospital bed.

GC, a *race car driver?*

I can't imagine it.

My grandma, a speed demon. And then I think about riding with her while she rips and screeches the minivan through the school carpool line, or squeezing my eyes closed and bracing myself when she runs yellow lights.

Maybe I *can* imagine it.

It's actually sort of cool. And I feel unique for the first time in my life. I am positive I am the only one in Treasure Valley Middle School who has a famous race car driver grandmother. Maybe even in the entire state of Arizona.

Why is this a secret? Does Mom know about this? I call her again. "Did you know Grandma is famous?"

"What?"

"Grandma is on Netopedia," I explain. I have to be patient with her. This news may come as quite a shock.

"I imagine she is," says Mom. She's not shocked.

I am shocked that she isn't shocked. "You mean you know? You've known all along that Grandma is a famous racecar driver? And you never said anything?"

Mom sighs. "Sophie, this isn't really a good time to discuss this. Yes, I know that your Grandma was a racecar driver. But that was a long time ago, before she was even married. It's not important now. I've got to go."

She hangs up before I can protest that it is actually very important. I am the granddaughter of someone famous and I didn't even know it. I am somebody. Sophie Murphy exists. When GC dies, people will notice that she's gone. They'll leave teddy bears in our front yard. When I go out in public, I will dress in black and cover my face with a scarf because I don't want them to see my swollen eyes. People will look at me and think, "That poor girl, I bet she'll miss her famous grandmother."

I have a lot to think about. Enough that I may need to take a bath. Too bad there's no one here to make bacon because that would help a lot with this process.

CHAPTER 55

Day 80. Fried Chicken

In the morning Ollie leaps onto my stomach to wake me up. We wander into the kitchen, where we find some frosted Os for breakfast. I really miss GC, and not just for her breakfasts. Her food is good, and I miss it, but most of all I miss her smell, her smile, and the sound of her voice even more. She just makes everything warm and comfy.

"How is she?" I ask Mom when she calls at ten.

"She's demanding fried chicken and Dr. Pepper," says Mom.

I laugh and feel the weight on my chest lift. "Better then."

"Her heart is not great," warns Mom. "But yes, if she keeps yelling they may just kick her out of here."

"Can I see her?" I ask.

"Not today. Wait until tomorrow."

I sigh. All this waiting is hard work. It could try a person's patience.

Mom gives me a look when she walks in the door that night. The look says "go away, I can't deal with you right now."

I ignore it. "Talk," I say. "Tell me the news."

She walks into the family room and drops to the couch, her arms and legs flat as if she were dead. "I don't know. They've opened up some veins to her heart, but it looks like a part of it died during the heart attack. They're sending her home, but she's weak. She may never be the same."

I don't even care. I don't care if GC sits on the couch and never bakes another blueberry muffin. I don't care if she'll never be able to play soccer or kick a football. I don't care if I will never have GC's lasagna again. What's important is that GC will be here.

We bring her home on a sunny afternoon on the first Friday in January. She's pale and smells distinctly like hospital disinfectant but her eyes are bright blue. She says she's happy to be home. Mom and I tuck her into bed. I pull the shades, but the stubborn sunshine streams around the outline of the shades and makes its presence known. GC doesn't seem to care. She lays her head back and closes her eyes.

A motionless GC is new for me. Even worse, she's in her bed. At home. I have never seen her there before. It's like seeing a cat floating in a swimming pool, or maybe me in a ballet class: it just doesn't belong there.

"Don't bug her," warns Mom later when she sees me tiptoeing toward GC's closed door.

"I won't," I assure Mom. I really want to though. I want to bust through her door and demand that she tell me how and why she kept these secrets from me. I want to know all about what it's like to be certifiably famous. But when I silently turn the knob and open the door to GC's room, I see that she hasn't moved. Except for the rise and fall of her chest, she's a concrete statue. I realize that I can wait. Her secrets have been silent for 50 years. They can wait one more day.

I pace, and eat, and try to watch a movie with Ollie, but the hours crawl by until it's time for bed. And still, GC sleeps.

When I hear her start moving on Saturday morning, I rush into her room with great news. "Today is your lucky day, GC. I have recorded 16 episodes of *The Price is Right* for you. Sixteen hours of pure bliss ahead."

She's still in bed. "Yay," she says dully.

I expected her to be a little more excited about this news.

"Before we start sixteen hours of bliss," she says, "I need to visit my bathroom, and then I'd like to talk to you. Will you just sit and talk to me for a while?"

My ears perk up. Talk? I'm down to talk, as long as we discuss secrets or fame. Hers, not mine.

"Yes, that is me," she says twenty minutes later when she climbs back into bed. I've used the time to find our laptop and pull up her Netopedia page.

I'm a little bit angry. Excited, but still angry. "But why, GC? This is life-changing news, why would you keep it a secret?"

"It wasn't really a secret," she says. "It just wasn't important to share."

I feel like a balloon that has been pumped so full of air it's on the verge of exploding. "Not important? It wasn't important enough to share *with your only granddaughter* that you have a legitimate Netopedia account? That when you die, you'll be featured in the national obituaries and people will actually notice that you are gone?"

She looks at me with tired eyes. "Am I important to you, Sophie?"

She should know the answer to that. I nod. "One of the most important people in the whole world."

"How long have I been important to you?"

I search my brain for memories of GC. Even though she lives thousands of miles away, she is present in almost all of the important scenes in my life. I think of long summer days in Minnesota. Holidays in Arizona. Birthdays. Skinned knees (a lot), broken bones (once), mosquito bites, sicknesses.

"You've been important to me since I was born," I tell her.

"So I was important even before you knew anything about racing?"

"Yes," I admit. Obviously.

"And you love me because of who I am, not what I once did."

I nod slowly. She's laying a trap and I'm walking right into it.

"And that's the kind of love that matters. The other stuff—fame, Netopedia—that's not love. You love me, I matter to you. That alone makes my life a success.

Her words seep into my mind slowly, like a pancake absorbing maple syrup.

"And I'm sure your Dad thought the same way. His life was worthwhile because you, your Mom, Ollie, and Trevor loved him. Being truly loved by one person is more important than being known by the entire world."

"All right," I say. I don't really understand but I need some time to absorb this. My pancake brain has soaked up so much syrup it's soggy and incapable of thinking.

I lay on the other side of GC's bed and turn on the first episode of *The Price is Right*, but even before it starts, the gymnast shaving commercial blares into the still air. It infiltrates the little space left in my head.

My Netopedia quest began with this commercial. I think of gymnastics (my crotch is *still* sore), my singing career (which still makes me cringe a little), and my football-kicking days (which were actually sort of fun, but still a failure). I am a failure. Sophie Murphy *still* does not exist, at least where it counts.

"What is being famous like, GC?" I ask after a while.

"Hmmm?" She's dozing, not even paying attention to Drew Carey.

I repeat my question.

"Darlin, I have no doubt that you have the drive and the talent to be successful. If fame is your goal, you'll probably get there."

Her eyes crinkle as she looks at me. "Have you ever eaten an entire lemon cream cheese pie?"

I think she's off her rocker. Is she avoiding my question intentionally or is she just senile? I humor her. "No, GC. I haven't."

"Not even on your birthday?"

"Nope. The most I've ever eaten is two slices."

Suddenly it's something I can't live without. I search the freezer where GC has hidden treats but find no lemon cheesecake. I crave it all evening.

CHAPTER 56

Day 82. Lemon Cheesecake

I said before that I hate all surprises because I like to be prepared for what is coming. That's still true. But I may make an exception if it involves lemon cheesecake. When the doorbell rings a couple of days later, and a delivery guy is standing there holding a pie, I decide I was wrong.

For Sophie's tongue ONLY says a note on the top. *Here's to fame.*

I really like fame. And lemon cheesecake. I don't even bother to get a plate, I eat right out of the box. When the first taste of lemony goodness hits my tongue, I wonder how I ever lived without it.

After the fifth slice, I hate lemon cheesecake. But I have never eaten an entire pie before, and I sort of feel obligated because it's all mine. If Trevor sees it then it will be mine no longer. By the time GC shuffles into the kitchen, the box is almost empty.

"You ate it!"

"Yeah." I'm starting to feel sick. Not sick as in meningitis or one of those other horrible diseases that I had but can't remember the name of now. Sick as in *Ew, I might throw up.* Sick as in *I can't stand the smell of this cheesecake and I want to throw it against the wall and watch it splatter.*

I look to GC for help.

"Walk away," she wheezes over her oxygen pump. "Someone else, probably Trevor, will stumble upon it and think he can't live without it. And you'll laugh and know that you've given it up for something better."

I don't know what she's talking about, but my stomach hurts too bad to think. I limp to GC's bed because it's really comfortable. Especially when she's there.

We lay next to each other in silence and watch three episodes of *The Price is Right.* I'm so busy thinking that I don't even pay attention until I hear Drew Carey congratulating a bald chubby man on his double showcase win. I turn to see if GC saw it, but she's asleep.

Practical Rules for Life

10. *Sometimes just a little is better than a whole lot.*

CHAPTER 57

Day 86. Muddling

It's therapy day, which is not a good thing. I never wanted to go to therapy but Mom said I had to 'talk to someone about Dad." To be honest, I'd rather have talked to her, but she wasn't really available.

I still don't want to go, and neither does Trevor. We consider sitting at Denny's for two hours instead, but we both know that if we don't show, the receptionist will call Mom within five minutes.

I talk to Dr. Williams about birthdays, skinned knees and mosquito bites, and what I've discovered about GC. I tell him that I actually have a famous grandmother and ask if he wants my autograph. I'm only partially joking.

He doesn't laugh. Or ask for my autograph. Where is that man's sense of humor? "What have you discovered about your grandmother?"

"Well, it's pretty cool that she's Pinky Morgan. But that's not why I love her. I love her because she's GC."

"What about the rest of your family? Haven't they been there too? What are your feelings about them?"

I consider this. Ollie: easy. Of course, I love Ollie. Loving him is like loving your favorite teddy bear. Trevor: harder. I'm not mad at him anymore. He's been gone for most of the last year, but he was there when GC got sick, when it really mattered.

"Trevor handles things in his own way, doesn't he? Being gone is his *coping mechanism*."

Dr. Williams smiles. His eyes crinkle and he actually smiles. And I like him a tiny bit more. "And your mother?"

"She's been there too. She muddled through all of it with us."

"Shouldn't you give her some credit for that?"

I narrow my eyes at him. "Dr. Williams? Have you been talking to my mom? Did she ask you to say that?"

"Not at all."

But she does pay you, I think. I don't say it out loud because it sounds disrespectful and sort of mean. I'm suspicious of Dr. Williams. I think he and Mom could be collaborating against Trevor and me.

CHAPTER 58

Day 1. Another New Normal

When Trevor and I get home, Mom is in the kitchen. "I made lasagna."

"You what?" Both Trevor and I stare at her. Words like those have never come out of her mouth.

She laughs. "Don't worry, I followed Grandma's instructions."

I take a goopy green smoothie to GC's room. She wrinkles her nose at it but sips a little.

I put my hands on my hips. "I expect you will drink it all by the time I come back."

GC lays her head on her pillow. "One bad day and the entire family thinks they can order me around. Just you wait, missy. I'm not puttin' up with this for long."

I kiss her papery cheek. "Sounds great GC."

Trevor is fishing in the fridge when I get back to the kitchen. "Where's the ketchup?"

"Trevor. We're eating lasagna. You don't need ketchup with lasagna."

"Ketchup makes everything taste better." Trevor winks at me and whispers. "Especially your cooking."

I laugh. Mom pretends she didn't hear him, except that she yanks the ketchup bottle from his hand and stows it back in the refrigerator door.

The lasagna is actually edible.

"Wanna hear a joke?" Ollie asks us while we eat. "What's a fish without eyes? A f-sh."

Ollie looks at me expectantly. He's in preschool, and can't spell so I'm not sure he even understands the joke.

Mom doesn't care. She laughs. "Good one, Ollie."

I look around the table. Dad is missing, but our tree is still alive. Ollie, Trevor, Mom, and GC (of course) are still my family. We all may muddle differently, and we may not understand each other all the time, but at least we muddle together. That's something.

After dinner, I put my essay on Mom's pillow with a note.

Like Dad, you are leaves. And I'm glad you haven't dropped.

Love Sophie

Mom wakes me up late that night. "Sophie."

I open my eyes. "Yes?"

She sits on my bed and brushes the hair from my face. "I read your essay. I'm so proud of you. You're tough, you know that? Life knocks you down and you get right back up."

"I guess," I tell her. "Eventually."

I sit up and wrap my arms around her waist. And then I go back to sleep.

CHAPTER 59

Day 5. Back

On the first day of school after winter break, I am fifteen minutes early for the first time ever. I pull open the door, wave hello to Mr. Gomez, and turn left instead of my usual right. Left toward the trophy case. I bypass the sports area and head straight to the academic section, pass the math trophies and the geography bee plaque, and stop. The place where my plaque belongs is still empty.

"It is still at the engravers," says a voice from behind me. I don't even need to turn around to know that the voice belongs to Mr. Gomez. I knew that guy read minds. It's a good thing I have nothing to hide.

"It's very fortunate that you're here. We need to take a photo with all the first-place finishers. Can you meet here right after the lunch bell rings?"

My Language Arts class is on the other side of the building, so when I get to the trophy case, the other two winners are already there.

"Sophie, do you know Mario Gutierrez and Carter Griffin? Mario is our photography winner and Carter won our art category."

I wave at them. I've been feeling shy around Carter since he walked me home. I haven't really known what to say to him.

"Hey Sophie," Carter says, as Mr. Gomez lines us up for the photo. I stand next to Carter because we are about the same height.

"You're an artist too? Like your mom?"

He ducks his head, embarrassed. "No. I'm not nearly as good. But I like to draw."

"What did you draw? Wait, I don't even need to ask. You drew a rooster."

He grins. "Nope. Roosters are my mom's thing. Not mine. I drew a hand."

"Now smile," Mr. Gomez calls.

I grin at the camera. Not only will my name be forever inscribed on a plaque in the Treasure Valley Middle School trophy case, but there will be a photo of me standing next to Carter. That's definitely something to smile about.

"You did it!" He says as we walk to the lunchroom. "You're famous."

"Sort of," I admit. "It's not like I imagined. And I'm not on Netopedia. But that's ok." I glance at him. "You're sort of famous too! And you drew a hand?"

"Yeah, dumb isn't it? I'm fascinated by human bodies. I want to be a doctor when I grow up."

"You knew about Louis Pasteur," I remember.

He grins and goes to sit at the lunch table with his friends.

I sit at my regular table too. I split my brownie and hand half to Mia. She eyes the half still in my hand, and I hand it to her too.

"What if Maddie Miller died?" I ask.

Mia stares at me with wide eyes. "Maddie Miller died?"

It takes a lot of patience to be friends with that girl. "No, she didn't die," I say. "But what if she did? Would you be so sad that you'd lock yourself in your bedroom for the next year?"

"Nah," says Jessie. "I don't even like her anymore. She's so...yesterday."

CHAPTER 60

Day 5 (continued). Pink Peonies

The house is quiet when I get home from school that afternoon, and the stillness hits me like a soggy beach towel. Stillness is not good. I run into GC's room. She's curled on the bed facing the window on the opposite side of the room. I know she's alive because I see her breathing. I stand next to her and watch her until my stomach rumbles. GC twitches and I decide to let her RIP. Not RIP as the obituaries say, but rest in peace meaning that I should let her sleep without me staring at her.

I rummage through the fridge, lean against the counter, and crunch into an apple. A vase of daisies sits on the kitchen table, their heads bowed, petals scattered. I wander to Dad's den, where I see wobbly letters drawn into the dust on his desk. O-L-L-I-E. Someone might brush it off, but it won't be me. I won't erase Ollie's attempts to make his mark on the world.

I hear the shuffle of slippers on the tile floor and turn to see GC wobbling toward me. She's holding tight to her walker and moving slower than pistachio pudding but Pink Peony lipstick glistens on her lips.

I beam at her. "You're up."

She waves her hand. "Of course I'm up, it's 3:30 in the afternoon," she says. "I've been up since five this morning. Already ran a marathon and fed the homeless."

I glance at her slippers and oxygen tank and laugh.

"Ok, maybe not that," she says. "But I did walk to the mailbox. Took me two hours, but I got the mail." She reaches into the pocket of her cardigan and hands me a stack of mail.

"Yay!" I pump my arms above my head. I'm as interested in the mail as I am a geometry textbook, but I don't want to mess with her victory, so I grab it. It feels like a stack of boring bills, except a wrinkled blue envelope on the top where Murphy Family is printed in smudged ink.

I'm one of those Murphy people, so I open the envelope and pull out a card.

Dear Murphy Family,

You don't know me, but I want to tell you how sorry I am for your loss. A few years ago I was down on my luck and lost my house. I had been on the streets for a few weeks when my back tooth started to hurt. Since you have a dentist in the family, you probably don't know how that feels, but it was the worst pain I have felt in my life. I wasn't sleeping or eating because of it and I couldn't do anything to make it stay away. One dentist shooed me out of his waiting room. Some other dentists I went to said they'd pull it for money I didn't have. A friend told me to see Dr. Murphy, that he cared about people like me.

Dr. Murphy fixed my tooth. But more important, he treated me like a person. Even after I walked out of his office, he found me to make sure that I was ok. He didn't make a big fuss about it, but he came to check on me every once in a while. It makes a difference to know that one person cares if you live or die. Dr. Murphy did that for me, and I'm not the only one. He was a good man and I'm sure you'll miss him. I will too.

Sincerely,

Joseph Gower

I think of Mr. Gower and Carter's mom, and I realize: Dad accomplished Rule #5: If you want to be remembered after you die, you have to accomplish something important while you're alive.

He *did* important things. They were just *quiet* important things.

Pride and sadness crash down on me at the same time. I wrap my arms around GC and wait for them to shrink, and then I look up at her. "Want to help me hang a rooster painting in my room?"

CHAPTER 61

Day 5 (continued again). I exist. And I'm Important

Practical Rules for Life

11. A person can be notable without Netopedia.

Maddie Miller probably hates lemon cheesecake too, I think that night as I lie in my bed and stare at the glow-in-the-dark stars on my ceiling. Those stars have been in the same place since I was eight or nine. I was too short to reach so Dad stood on my bed and stuck each star to the ceiling as I pointed where it needed to go.

Stars.

Is sticking stars on a ceiling more important than singing love songs in front of screaming fans who like you one day and are finished with you the next? Is helping one man more important than flipping for a gold medal?

And then it occurs to me: my dad didn't even like teddy bears, so a pile at the doorstep wouldn't matter at all. But he loved me. And his life was important to me, to my family, and to Joseph Gower. He's not one of the Michael Murphys listed on Netopedia, but he still existed.

And I existed to him.

Sophie Murphy exists for GC, Mom, and Ollie (maybe Trevor too). And that's enough.

At least for now.

Sophie Murphy's Practical Rules for Life

1. When you feel overwhelmed by a huge thing, break it into baby things.

2. Be prepared. Surprises usually don't turn out well.

3. Do not eat 5 corndogs and then go to bed.

4. Do not, under any circumstance, ever eat an elephant. Even if you're on an African safari and the only dinner choices are hedgehogs or elephants.

5. If you want to be remembered after you die, you have to do something important while you're alive.

6. Avoid doing more than two summersaults in public.

7. Break eggs, not legs.

8. GC makes everything better.

9. Sometimes you have to change your plans. And rip up lists.

10. Sometimes just a little is better than a whole lot.

11. A person can be notable without Netopedia.

Acknowledgements

A number of people helped Sophie's story unfold, and my gratitude goes to them. Thanks to my children, who rolled their eyes but who patiently provided criticism and suggestions (mostly criticism); to Troy, for endless plot chats and editing suggestions; to generous beta readers Misty Summers, Rachel Page, Kirsten Bethers, Elizabeth Dunford, Thomas Dunford, Rachel Robins and Scott Blanchard.

A deep bow goes to Chicken Scratch Books and Kiri Jorgensen, whose ideas and suggestions made Sophie so much better. I'm grateful that she has a home with you.

There are good people in the world, some who work quietly without fanfare. Thanks to those who are examples of kindness and who inspired characters in the story. To my parents, Ted and Sandi McDaniel; neighbors and friends Dan and Kirsten Bethers, Kevin and Alisa Childs—I see you.

ABOUT THE AUTHOR

Tiffany Blanchard lives with her husband and four children in the red rocks of southern Utah. She spends her days practicing law, running, and losing to her children in challenges and card games. This is her first novel.

Chicken Scratch Reading School

Sophie Murphy Does Not Exist
Novel Study Course

www.chickenscratchbooks.com/courses

Join us at **Chicken Scratch Reading School** for an online Novel Study Course for *Sophie Murphy Does Not Exist*. Created by certified teachers with extensive curriculum design experience, this offering is a full 6-week course of study for 5th-8th grade students. It includes reading study focus, quizzes, vocabulary work, thematic and writing device analysis, a written essay, and culmination project. The course includes a mix of online and on-paper work, highlighted by instructional **VIDEOS** from the author, Tiffany Blanchard, and publisher Kiri Jorgensen.

Chicken Scratch Books creates online novel study courses for each book we publish. Our goal is to teach our readers to appreciate strong new traditional literature.

At Chicken Scratch Books,
Traditional Literature is all we do.

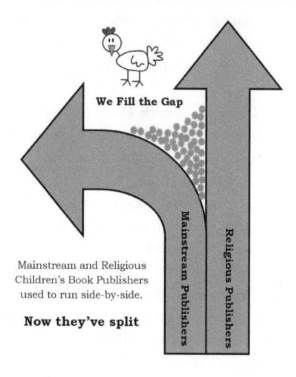

We Fill the Gap

Mainstream Publishers

Religious Publishers

Mainstream and Religious
Children's Book Publishers
used to run side-by-side.

Now they've split

www.chickenscratchbooks.com